KARATE
Zen, Pen, and Sword

by
Randall G. Hassell

EMPIRE Books
P.O. Box 491788, Los Angeles, CA 90049

Disclaimer
Please note that the author and publisher of this book are NOT RESPONSIBLE in any manner whatsoever for any injury that may result from practicing the techniques and/or following the instructions given within. Since the physical activities described herein may be too strenuous in nature for some readers to engage in safely, it is essential that a physician be consulted prior to training.

Published in 2006 by Empire Books.
Copyright © 2006 by Randall G. Hassell

All rights reserved. No part of this publication may be reproduced or utilized in any form or by any means, electronic or mechanical, including photocopying, recording, or by any information storage and retrieval system, without prior written permission from Empire Books.

Library of Congress Number: 2006010643
ISBN-10: 1-933901-16-0
ISBN-13: 978-1-933901-16-9

Library of Congress Cataloging-in-Publication Data

Hassell, Randall G.
Karate : zen, pen and sword / by Randall G. Hassell. -- 1st ed.
p. cm.
Includes index.
ISBN 1-933901-16-0 (pbk. : alk. paper)
1. Karate--Philosophy. 2. Karate--Psychological aspects. I. Title.
GV1114.3.H399 2006
796.815'201--dc22
2006010643

Empire Books
P.O. Box 491788
Los Angeles, CA 90049
(818) 767-9000

06 05 04 03 02 01 00 99 98 97 1 3 5 7 9 10 8 6 4 2

Printed in the United States of America

Dedication

For Charles O. Bauer II and Dale F. Poertner, mentors, critics, editors, friends. "So filled with life, even death was caught off-guard."

Contents

PART I—ZEN
    Strength 1
    Self-Preservation. 1
    Killing 2
    Warriors of Life. 2
    The "No Hands" School. 2
    Fighting with Wolves 4
    A Good Pupil. 4
    Trading Life for Enlightenment. 4
    Don't Think, Just Do 6
    The Meaning of *Do* 6
    Empty Your Cup 7
    True Wealth. 7
    Awareness 8
    Emptiness 8
    How to Master the Spear 9
    Obedience 10
    Great Waves 10
    The First Principle 11
    Heaven and Hell 12
    Temper 13
    True Mastery. 14
    Spirit First, Techniques Second. 15
    The Secret of Swordsmanship 17
    What You See is What You Believe 18
    Perspective 20
    Do What Must be Done 21
    You Cannot Attack Emptiness 22
    Fate 23
    An Enlightened Man. 24

Delicious 24
A Whack on the Head. 25
A Real Teacher 25

PART II—PEN
What is Karate?. 27
Technique (*Jutsu*) and Art (*Do*) 34
Psychological Principles. 36
Kinesthesia 41
Karate and Physical Fitness 44
Karate as a Point of View 48
Centering 51
Zen and *Bushido*: The Great Empty Circle 56
Karate-do and Personality 60
Stress and Anxiety 76
Samurai Strategy 81
The Karate Experience: A Way of Life 87
The Positive Lifestyle 91

PART II—SWORD
Meeting Myself 99
Entering the Way 100
Starting Over 102
Don't Run 105
A True Master 107
Karate Ni Sente Nashi 109
If a Nail Sticks Up, Hammer it Down 112
Haragei—Speaking from the Gut 114
Discretion is the Better Part of Valor 116
If It's Non-Contact, How Do You Know It Will Work? . . 118
Use Your Brain (When You Are Supposed To). 123
Now I Know 123

About the Author

Martial Arts Illustrated magazine called Randall G. Hassell "Shotokan's Great Communicator" and "The spiritual voice for a generation of karate-do practitioners." *The Fighter International* magazine said Hassell is, "hands down, the world's finest, most authoritative karate-do writer."

Chief Instructor of the American Shotokan Karate Alliance (ASKA), President of the American JKA Karate Association International (AJKA-I), and Senior Editor of Tamashii Press, Randall Hassell is a professional writer and editor who began karate training in 1960. He also is a first generation American to pioneer Shotokan karate, introducing it to the St. Louis, Missouri area in 1961.

While majoring in English Literature at Washington University in St. Louis, he began an intense, formal study of the history and philosophy of the martial arts in general, and karate-do in particular.

To date, this study has led to the publication of more than 100 articles in numerous periodicals around the world, and more than 28 books including:
The Complete Idiot's Guide to Karate; Recognition: A Karate Novel (with Stan Schmidt)*; The Karate Experience: A Way of Life; Conversations with the Master: Masatoshi Nakayama; Shotokan Karate: Its History and Evolution; Karate Ideals; The Karate Spirit ; Karate Training Guide Volume 1: Foundations of Training; Karate Training Guide Volume 2: Kata—Heian, Tekki, Bassai Dai; Samurai Journey (*with Osamu Ozawa*).

In addition to teaching in his own dojo and at various YMCAs and school districts in the St. Louis, Missouri metro area, Mr. Hassell oversees the instruction and administration of thousands of students nationwide in ASKA and AJKA affiliated clubs, and he travels extensively, teaching, lecturing, and officiating.

Preface

Almost 30 years ago, I wrote *The Karate Experience, A Way of Life*. This little, autobiographical/philosophical book was issued in hardback by the Charles E. Tuttle Company, and to my great delight, remained in print in its original form for almost 12 years. Because of numerous requests from around the world, I considered having *The Karate Experience* re-issued, but everything has its useful life and then must pass on. This, I believe, is the case with *The Karate Experience*.

My decision, therefore, was to use parts of *The Karate Experience* as a foundation for expanding on the basic thoughts presented there and presenting them to a wider audience than was considered the first time around.

The "Zen" section of this book, therefore, contains re-tellings of timeless traditional stories that I believe are essential to an understanding of the role of Zen in the martial arts. The "Pen" section is a compilation of expositions (intellectual exercises) on the nature of karate-do and contains revisions of much of the material found in *The Karate Experience*. The "Sword" section is a collection of modern stories of the exploits and deeds of modern practitioners.

With the exception of "Meeting Myself" in the Sword section (which recounts true, deeply personal events in my own life), I cannot attest to the truth or validity of any of the stories in this book. Whether they are true or not is, in fact, irrelevant. My only criteria for including them were, "Is this story significant, and is it likely to have a significant impact?" In the case of legends, truth often is not a good measure of significance.

Timeless stories of sensational exploits and extraordinary deeds abound in the martial arts, but because most of them have been transmitted orally through generations, they have gone virtually undocumented. Of the hundreds of books and thousands of magazine articles written about the martial arts, no more than a handful of these fascinating historical accounts has appeared in print. This book contains a collection of provocative anecdotes, both modern and ancient, each of which depicts, through the philosophy and actions of martial arts masters and Zen masters, how people have overcome obstacles and resolved conflicts in dealing with other people.

The stories presented here, whether factual or fictional, are immortal because they provide important lessons not confined by time or territory. The themes—peace and violence, strength and weakness, love and hate, and so on—are universal. Within each saga can be found a moral—usually one that can be applied to broader spheres of day-to-day life, human relationships, and survival.

Martial art, in its highest form, is a holistic practice of spiritual, intellectual, and physical dimensions. Symbolically, then, Zen represents the spiritual dimension, pen represents the intellectual dimension, and sword represents the physical dimension of the martial arts in general, and karate-do in particular. Further, the problems appearing in each story are resolved through the means of one and sometimes all three ingredients of Zen, pen, and sword.

While I must speak primarily about karate-do, because that is what I know best, this book is for all martial artists, regardless of art, rank, style, or political affiliation.

Randall G. Hassell
St. Louis, Missouri

Introduction

• • • • • • • • • • • • • • • **ZEN** • • • • • • • • • • • • • • •

Two Zen monks were walking down a muddy road in the rain when they came upon a beautiful young woman, dressed in exquisite clothes, standing at a river crossing.

Without saying a word, the older of the two monks scooped the young woman up in his arms and carried her across the river.

When they reached the end of their journey, the younger monk lost control. "How could you do such a thing?" he demanded indignantly. "We are monks with Buddhist vows of celibacy and rectitude. You know it is forbidden to gaze upon a beautiful young woman, much less touch her! This kind of thing is dangerous to the doctrines! It is against all our principles! What's wrong with you?"

Replied the older monk calmly, "I put the girl down at the roadside. Are you still carrying her?"

* * * * *

Zen is a concept that was brought to China from India by Bodhidharma in about 600 A.D., and after all these centuries, it still defies definitive definition.

Indeed, the best definition of Zen lies in what it is not. Zen is not a philosophy, nor is it a religion. It has no universal creed or dogma, and its practitioners are not required to enter into monastic vows. It seeks no salvation, and it offers no rewards to the faithful. Many practitioners of Zen, of course, have offered definitions based on their own, individual understanding, and some have created creeds and doctrines that fit the circumstances of their lives. But no matter how detailed we get, or how "expert" we become, we have little hope of finding a better definition of Zen than is found in the teaching of the great masters: Zen is eating when we are hungry, sleeping when we are tired, and breathing when we are alive.

But we all do this, protests the intellectual. Yes, but according to the Zen masters, we don't really do these things as much as we just let them happen. There is a significant difference.

The spirit of Zen practice is effort, willpower, and self-reliance. Zen is the positive, active pursuit of *really* eating, *really* sleeping, and *really* breathing. This spirit defies logic, reason, and analysis. It is, above all, direct awareness of reality through direct action. Zen rejects intellectualizing in favor of a flashbulb awareness of truth. The essence of Zen is, "Don't think; just do."

The old monk who carried the girl across the river is a perfect example of Zen in action. Even though he violated his vows, his heart was pure, and his mind was clear. He did not think about the act at all; he simply did it and moved on.

In the modern world, outside the martial arts, we can see the essence of Zen in infants and young children. When a ball is rolled to an infant, the child sees no separation between itself and the ball. Infants are completely "in" the experience of the rolling ball. They perceive no difference between themselves and the experience of the rolling ball. Their grasp of their world is immediate and direct, and this is why we can roll the ball to a child again and again, with no abatement of joy or enthusiasm on the part of the child. The more the intellect develops, however, the less joy there is to be found in the experience of the rolling ball. As adults, we look at the rolling ball and simply express our intellectual understanding that the round thing is a ball and that it will roll on the floor if given a push. We separate ourselves from the experience.

The direct, immediate approach of Zen was very appealing to the samurai of old, and it was natural that they would seek

Zen training for two important reasons: (1) Zen calls for direct action without thought and without looking back, and (2) it proposes that the enlightened person is utterly indifferent to life and death. Both of these ideas are very appealing to warriors who are facing death on the battlefield.

What Zen proposes is that it is better to empty the mind of all its illusions—guilt, fear, doubt, greed, and so on—and to directly experience each event in life as the child experiences a rolling ball. In short, it enables a person to be a part of the action as the action actually is and to respond to any situation in accord with the universal laws of nature. When the mind thinks about one thing or another, it "stops" on that point, and awareness is lost. As the master Takuan pointed out in his famous treatise on the subject, "When I look at a tree, I perceive one of the leaves is red, and my mind 'stops' with this leaf. When this happens, I see just one leaf and fail to take notice of the innumerable other leaves of the tree. If instead of this I look at the tree without any preconceived ideas, I shall see all the leaves. One leaf effectively 'stops' my mind from seeing all the rest. But when the mind moves on without 'stopping,' it takes up hundreds of thousands of leaves without fail."

The non-stopping mind is called *mushin*, which means "empty mind." But this empty state of mind is not empty in the sense of mindless or ignorant; rather, it is empty in the sense that a circle is empty. It is at once empty and complete, like a great empty circle. It is completely functional and fulfilled. What the empty mind is empty of is preconceived notions, emotions, aimless thoughts, fear, doubt, guilt, and hatred.

A samurai who attained *mushin* could therefore face his opponents with a completely clear and "empty" mind. He would show no fear in the face of the enemy, and he was utterly indifferent to the prospect of death.

Paradoxically, then, the "spiritual" side of the martial arts—Zen—is a striving against the intellect. It is a discipline that leads the practitioner toward a state in which the mind moves freely, unencumbered by emotional blockades and feelings of fear and anxiety. It is a state of mind that enables martial artists to see their opponents as they actually are and, like Takuan seeing all the leaves on the tree, missing nothing.

The concept of *mushin* is also appealing to modern martial artists who seek to master their art and protect themselves from danger. It enables martial artists to respond naturally and instantaneously to any threat. Even the most physically skilled athlete or master martial artist will be injured or killed if, when a mugger suddenly attacks with a lead pipe, the mind is allowed to stop and deliberate on the proper response. The mugger has the physical and strategic advantage, and even the slightest delay on the part of the martial artist will result in defeat. Through Zen training and diligent training in techniques, the martial artist will be able to circumvent the intellect and respond like (as Zen masters say) "flint striking steel." There will not be even a hint of a pause between perception of the attack and the proper response.

When the mind has been completely emptied through Zen practice and centered in the whole body, which has been thoroughly strengthened through martial arts training, the body and mind will respond as one unit. The legs will go where they are supposed to go, and the arms will do their work without any conscious command.

To describe the spiritual nature of modern arts, we use the word *do*. *Do* (pronounced as in "bread dough") means "way" or "path," and it implies that the martial art is used as a vehicle for traveling the path that leads to a correct and fulfilling life. Today there are relatively few martial arts teachers in the West who purport to be "leading in the way." The vast majority are too concerned with technical proficiency to be bothered with spiritual insight. Nevertheless, mere technical achievement will not automatically manifest itself in an understanding of *do*;

neither will mere meditation provide one with superior physical skills.

This is evident in the stories in this book. In the tradition of *do*, the stories often reflect the striving for spiritual perfection through physical training. This is as it should be. Martial artists who seek spiritual awakening must seek it actively and must keep themselves open to accepting it when it appears.

The main thing that must be noted is that the process of attaining spiritual awakening (enlightenment) in the martial arts is not a process of intellectualizing or understanding with the mind. It is the process of solving a problem that cannot be solved with the intellect. In the Zen tradition, such a problem is called a *koan*, and it is a seemingly unsolvable problem that remains unsolvable as long as the student seeks the answer through intellect. But the solution is simple: it is always found in intuitive insight that springs from hard, continuous, physical training. It is so simple that anyone can understand it, but it is so difficult to experience that few achieve it. In every case, awakening comes when students are able to solve the *koan* without their intellect. They must directly experience the answer and delve ever more deeply into the nature of life.

This is the essence of Zen in the martial arts.

PEN

Kenzenichi is a Japanese maxim, which means that the sword (or fist) and the writing brush are one and the same. It is a high ideal that has been expressed throughout hundreds of years of literature, and it is as confusing and difficult now as it was for the samurai of old.

While Zen symbolizes the spiritual nature of the martial ways, the pen, or writing brush, symbolizes the intellectual side.

In Zen we have the paradox of trying to reach true understanding without using the mind. With the pen we have the paradox of trying to develop the intellect without defeating our spiritual goals. On the surface, this is indeed a difficult problem.

For the samurai, it was not as difficult a problem as it is for us today. From birth, samurai children were schooled in the classics. They were taught in fine schools, and were forced to be excellent students. When they attained a certain level of maturity, they then were trained in the ways of the warrior, and they sought enlightenment. Today, however, Westerners are faced with the problem of trying to learn their arts while at the same time trying to learn the history and philosophy of the East. The body and mind are placed under great stress. Many of us, of course, simply eliminate the intellectual side of the martial arts in favor of more technical proficiency.

This is an unfortunate state of affairs.

There are two ways in which to consider the pen as the intellectual side of the martial arts; one way is technical, and the other way is purely intellectual.

The technical way of the pen in Asia is calligraphy. The Japanese and Chinese look at the calligraphy of martial artists to determine their state of mind and depth of understanding.

Bearing in mind that the essence of Zen is to let the mind move freely, without stopping, the calligraphy is studied to determine how well the Zen process is working.

The purpose of the non-stopping mind is to flow freely, perceiving everything at once. When martial artists face an opponent, they try to maintain, through an empty and flowing mind, a state of continuous awareness. They strive to keep their entire being—body, mind, and spirit—in harmonious balance, offering the opponent no opening for attack. When the mind stops or even hesitates, an opening, or *suki*, appears. Literally, *suki* means "a space between two things." It is the *suki* that the mind of *mushin* seeks to avoid, and it is the *suki* that the empty mind will attack in the opponent. In the martial arts, *suki* is the crucial instant between inhalation and exhalation. In calligraphy, it is the crucial instant when the brush touches the paper for the first time, and it is called *raku-hitsu*.

A single stroke of the brush (pen) indicates the state of the martial artist's development, both spiritually and intellectually. Too much concentration at the beginning of the stroke cause the stroke to trail off weakly; thinking about the end makes the beginning weak. Thinking about the beginning and the end makes the middle weak; and thinking about the whole stroke inevitably makes the stroke too large or too small. Only when the mind moves freely, without thinking or stopping at all, can the entire stroke be made smoothly, with consistency, uniformity, and proper proportion. A martial artist may, therefore, appear to move freely and smoothly in action, but fail the test of the pen. Traditionally, both are necessary; both must be the same.

The "purely intellectual" way of the pen in the martial arts is, like all other aspects of the traditional ways, a paradox in itself. In the traditional ways, it has always been incumbent on the teachers to pass along the knowledge and truth of their arts to their students. These truths are usually confusing, secret transmissions (called *hiden* in Japanese) which, when written, are unintelligible without verbal and physical elaboration.

The *hiden* are the touchstones of understanding, written down and passed from master to master, which provide the keys to the *koan* the students encounter in training. Again, like all other aspects of the martial ways, they defy logic, reason, and intellect. They are, like the stories in this book, little vignettes that create a spark in the mind, which must be translated first into action and then into intuitive understanding.

Every master of the martial ways has their own *koan* to solve if they desire to transmit their *hiden* to future generations. The *koan* is: Whatever the motive for writing—profit, transmission of secrets, amusement, admiration of your peers—that motive will be reflected in the writing, and the writing will not be done in a state of *mushin*. If, however, there is no motive for writing, how do you begin to write?

This is the essence of the pen in the martial arts.

• • • • • • • • • • • • • • SWORD • • • • • • • • • • • • • •

Because action speaks louder than words and lends itself to graphic literary portrayal, all the stories in this book are depicted in physical circumstances. Physical feats, especially those performed cleverly or spectacularly, leave a lasting impression. Concrete—as opposed to abstract—devices, notably, can be integrated with spiritual or intellectual elements to make a profound statement to even the most casual reader. It works perfectly here, since the physical dimension of the martial arts is recognizable by just about everyone today.

Because martial artists' hands and feet are their swords, the word "sword" is applied in its symbolic context. Seldom is an actual weapon used in these stories.

Many of the accounts vividly describe close encounters of the physical kind. In many cases, the uninitiated reader may believe that the means employed to reach a resolution are brutal, violent, and unjustified. It is therefore imperative to elaborate on the psychological nature of martial arts masters and instructors, and the extreme difference between how the arts were once taught and how they are taught today.

Originally, the Asian martial arts were military disciplines and an integral part of the warrior's training. They also were taught by warrior-priests in China and Japan who, in the course of spreading God's word, were equally adept at sending an enemy to the devil. By the late 19th century, many of these warlike arts evolved into disciplines embracing spiritual and philosophic connotations. Hence, contrasting methods of self-preservation and self-realization exist even today. The aspect emphasized depends on the conviction of the person teaching the art.

Those who subscribe to the self-preservation concept usually learned their arts in the 1950s and 1960s from severe taskmasters under unbelievably ruthless conditions. Accordingly, such men conduct their own classes with absolute military discipline and uncompromising brutality. Even in America, the scene of many stories in this book, the rigid methods continued until the early 1970s. From Bruce Lee's films and TV's Kung Fu series to the films of Chuck Norris, Steven Seagal, and Teenage Mutant Ninja Turtles, martial arts have captivated the masses, and an unprecedented influx of new students has turned the martial arts into big business.

Before the early 1970s, the martial arts retained a lot of mystique. The "karate expert" was generally believed capable of killing anyone with one deadly "chop." This attitude wasn't totally unjustified. The early group of pioneers who established karate in the United States, from 1946 onward, were a rugged lot. The Americans were ex-servicemen who had learned the arts while stationed in Asia. The Asian pioneers, sent by parent schools in their native country, were survivalists of the first order.

This stalwart group of black belts overcame enormous obstacles in transplanting their arts in America. Many people questioned the effectiveness of these disciplines because so many incredible tales surrounded them. Challenges from rough-and-tumble street fighters were frequent. In dealing with these problems, the early black belts became renowned for making converts of skeptics.

Thus, the martial arts instructor (always male in those days) emerged as a figure of physical superiority. Within his school, he was accorded absolute allegiance. His every word was gospel, and his authority in matters in and out of the martial arts was never questioned. His classes were better defined as survival courses. Students were physically beaten, grossly humiliated, and driven to inhumane states of exhaustion.

These indignities were understood and accepted by students of the "old school." The actions that today would result in lawsuits were then everyday training methods. Devotees who survived the training acquired deep personal insights.

Because they deal with life and death, martial artists subscribe to a strict code of conduct. An expert might use physical force in any one of three situations: self-defense, instruction, or for the protection of others. The extent to which an expert becomes physical is based on each situation's conditions. In accordance with warrior ethics, an expert might act with swift and sudden violence when provoked. To the uninitiated reader, these actions might appear unaccountably violent; to the warrior martial artist, the retaliation is justified.

ZEN

Strength

One day, as a Zen master strolled through a field with his student, a pheasant started from a nearby bush, and, in fright, darted awkwardly into a thicket. Seeking to impress the master with his powers of observation, the student, with sarcastic certainty, remarked, "Birds are so weak and defenseless!"

The Zen master swung his walking staff and rapped the student sharply across the shins.

"Fly!" he commanded.

Self-Preservation

A Zen master out for a walk with one of his students pointed out a fox chasing a rabbit.

"According to an ancient fable, the rabbit will get away from the fox," the master said.

"Not so," replied the student. "The fox is faster."

"But the rabbit will elude him," insisted the master.

"Why are you so certain?" asked the student.

"Because the fox is running for his dinner, and the rabbit is running for his life," answered the master.

Killing

The Zen master, Gasan, one day told his disciples, "Killing is wrong. We should never kill as the warriors do. We should not even kill insects. But the warriors are not the most vicious killers. The most vicious killers are those hypocrites who rail against killing but continually kill time, squander money, and kill the economy of the nation."

"The worst killers of all," he said, "are those who teach Zen without enlightenment. They are killing the Buddha himself."

Warriors of Life

A group of army officers who were on maneuvers with their men one day took over the temple of Gasan, the Zen master, as a temporary field headquarters.

At dinner time, Gasan loudly told the cook, "Don't fix anything special. These men should eat the same food we do."

"Who do you think you're talking to?" one indignant samurai asked Gasan. "We are great warriors, sacrificing everything for the benefit of our country!"

"Who do you think you're talking to?" replied Gasan. "We are warriors of mankind, sacrificing everything for the benefit of humanity!"

The "No Hands" School

Tsukahara Bokuden, one of Japan's greatest swordsmen, was one day crossing Lake Biwa in a rowboat with a number of other passengers. One of them, a tough-looking samurai, was boasting about his skill with the sword. He said he was the best in the land, and that no one could defeat him.

While all the other passengers were paying close attention to the man, Bokuden was leaning back, dozing, as if the man were not even there. Angered by Bokuden's nonchalance, the samurai shook him and said, "You have two swords, but pay no attention. What's your problem?"

"My art is different from yours," replied Bokuden. "It doesn't care about defeating opponents, but rather cares about not being defeated."

"What silly school is that?" asked the samurai.

"It is the 'no hands' school," said Bokuden. "We only carry a sword to perfect our character, not to kill people."

"Is that so?" bellowed the angry samurai. "Do you really think you could defeat me without using your hands—without drawing your sword?"

"Sure," replied Bokuden confidently.

At this, they agreed to a duel, and Bokuden directed the boatman to row to a far island in the middle of the lake so that they could fight without anyone else getting in the way.

When they reached the island, the braggart samurai leapt off the boat and drew his sword, ready to kill Bokuden the moment he disembarked.

Bokuden slowly took off his own swords and handed them to the boatman. Then, just as he was about to step off the boat, he grabbed the boatman's oar and, pushing it hard against the ground, propelled the boat backwards into deep water.

Rowing away from the bewildered man on the shore, Bokuden called out, "This is my 'no hands' school!"

Fighting with Wolves

A pack of vicious wolves began prowling a village near the temple of the Zen master, Shoju, and the villagers were terrified. Hearing about it, Shoju went to the local graveyard and sat there in meditation all night, every night for one week. To the surprise of everyone, the wolves disappeared. The villagers were so happy and amazed, that they went to Shoju and begged him to tell them the secret of defeating wolves.

"There is no secret and no technique," said Shoju. "I simply sat in meditation with a clear and empty mind. The wolves would gather around me, licking my face, bumping my throat with their noses, and sniffing at my body. But because I kept an empty mind and a steady demeanor, they didn't bite. This is what I am always preaching to you: if you will practice, you will be able to move freely between earth and heaven, invulnerable even to wolves. I just practice what I preach."

A Good Pupil

According to the Zen master, Gasan, there are three types of pupils: "A bad pupil tells everyone the name of his master and brags. An average pupil expresses admiration for his master's knowledge and kindness. A good pupil says nothing and grows strong under his master's discipline."

Trading Life for Enlightenment

In both Zen and martial arts, students are expected to follow their teacher no matter what the teacher does, and no matter how severely they are treated. In the Zen tradition, students of some masters are required to make a blood oath that they will obey the master even if he kills them.

One master, Ekido, was severe in the extreme. His students were so scared of him that they were not progressing properly. One day, Ekido observed a student watching a pretty girl walking past the temple. The student was striking the gong to announce the time of day, and because of his wandering eye, he missed a beat.

Ekido, who was standing behind the student, hit him hard on the head with a stick, and the student died instantly from the shock.

The next day, the student's father came to Ekido and thanked him for being such a good and fair master. He praised him for his strict adherence to the correct path.

While most Zen masters are lucky to produce even one enlightened successor, it is said that after this incident, Ekido produced more than 10.

Don't Think, Just Do

The Zen disciple, Inzan, one day went before his master, Gasan, to give an answer for his *koan*. Before Inzan could say anything, Gasan held out his hand and asked, "Why is this called a hand?" Before Inzan could answer, Gasan kicked out at him and asked," Why is this called a leg?"

As Inzan opened his mouth to reply, Gasan clapped his hands and laughed loudly. So perplexed was Inzan by all of this that he bowed and silently left the room.

The next day Gasan said to him, "These are loose times for Zen. The practitioners skip lightly over the *koan*, and they jump at all chances to write comments and poems. Everybody wants to be an 'expert,' but nobody is willing to submit to the

proper discipline. No matter how times and people change, there is still only one way to obtain Zen: You must put aside everything you have ever heard or done, and fill yourself with one purpose only. It is absolutely necessary to die and be reborn."

It is said that upon hearing those words, Inzan attained enlightenment.

The Meaning of *Do*

The Zen master, Kaishu, was crossing a river one day in a boat with several pupils. It was raining violently, and the waves were tossing the boat to and fro. As the storm worsened, several of the young Buddhists became so frightened that they cried and shouted prayers to Avalokitesvara, the Buddhist goddess of love.

All the while, Kaishu sat calmly in meditation, breathing evenly and smiling faintly.

When the boat reached the shore, one of the pupils blurted out, "Sensei, weren't you scared?"

Said Kaishu, giggling, "A man is worthless if he can't take care of himself and let his *Do* sustain him in bad times. The goddess must be laughing herself silly at all of you."

Empty Your Cup

Nan-in, a great Zen master, one day granted an audience to a college professor who wanted to learn something about Zen.

While pouring tea, Nan-in continued pouring tea in the man's cup until the cup was completely full, and tea was spilling all over the table.

Somewhat disturbed by this, the professor finally shouted, "The cup is too full! You're wasting that tea!"

Nan-in replied, "Just like this cup, you are too full of your own ideas and illusions. I can teach you nothing until you empty your cup."

True Wealth

A very rich man approached the Zen master, Sengai, and asked him to write a poem or a prayer in praise of the continued wealth and affluence of his family.

Sengai wrote, "Father dies, son dies, grandson dies."

Upon reading this, the rich man angrily flung the paper at Sengai and shouted, "I ask you for an heirloom, and you treat it as a lark! What is this trifling nonsense?"

"I did not take your request lightly," replied Sengai. "You see, if your son dies before you do, you will be deeply grieved. And if your grandson dies first, both you and your son will feel grief beyond measure. But if your family, from generation to generation, dies in the order I have indicated, it will be following the true and natural course of life and death. That is true wealth."

Awareness

Tsukahara Bokuden, one of Japan's greatest swordsmen, wanted to test the abilities of his three sons, all of whom had trained in the way of the samurai. To do this, Bokuden placed a pillow over the curtain on the door to his room, so that when the curtain was raised, the pillow would fall on the head of the person entering—a very unpleasant experience for that person, because pillows in Japan were made of solid wood.

Bokuden first called his oldest son, who saw the pillow, took it down, entered the room, and replaced the pillow over the curtain.

As the second son entered, the pillow fell, but he caught it in his hands and placed it back over the curtain.

As the youngest son rushed in, the pillow fell squarely on his head, but he cut it in half with his sword before it hit the floor.

To the first son, Bokuden gave his sword, saying, "You are a great swordsman."

To the second son he said, "You will one day become a great swordsman, but you must yet train very hard."

To the third son he said, "You are a disgrace to this family, and are not qualified to even hold a sword."

So saying, he took his youngest son's sword away from him and cast him out of the house.

Emptiness

One day as Dokuon, the great Zen master, was idly smoking his long, bamboo pipe, he was approached by Tesshu, a famous samurai who was studying Zen. Tesshu exclaimed ecstatically that he had finally grasped the essence of true *kara*. He was finally empty, he said. The universe is empty, there is no difference between subjective and objective, and so on.

Expressionless, Dokuon listened quietly for a few minutes, and then suddenly smacked Tesshu sharply on the head with his pipe.

Enraged, the swordsman leapt to his feet and shouted, "You stupid old fool! That hurt! I could kill you for that!"

"My, my," said Dokuon calmly, "This emptiness is certainly quick to show anger, isn't it?"

Presently, Tesshu smiled sheepishly and crept away.

How to Master the Spear

Yasuoki was a great warrior who specialized in the use of the spear. Nothing incensed him more than hearing about the presence of mind of the Zen masters.

To test the validity of the stories and to dispel what he felt were hateful rumors, he invited the great Zen master, Bankei, to visit him.

While he and Bankei were chatting and sipping tea, Yasuoki suddenly grabbed his spear and thrust it violently at Bankei.

With seeming nonchalance, Bankei diverted the head of the spear with his rosary and said, "Tsk, tsk. Lousy technique. You're too excited."

Following this encounter, Yasuoki became the greatest spearsman in Japan, and he always said that Bankei was the *sensei* who taught him the most about his art.

Obedience

The Zen master, Bankei, was somewhat of a rebel among the masters of his day. He refused to teach in the accepted fashion, preferring instead to just open his mind to his disciples and say whatever came to him.

A priest from another sect was perturbed by the large audiences Bankei drew, and he decided to test him during one of Bankei's lectures.

"Bankei!" he shouted out, "You have no true disciples, because true disciples are brought up correctly in the way, and they will obey their master. No one in his right mind would obey you!"

"Come up to the front," said Bankei, "and I will show you how I make people obey."

The haughty priest sauntered up, and Bankei said, "Okay, stand over here on my right."

The priest stood on the right.

"No, sorry," said Bankei. "It will work better if you are on my left."

The priest moved to Bankei's left.

"There," said Bankei. "First right and then left. You have obeyed me perfectly. Now sit down, shut up, and listen."

Great Waves

One of Japan's most famous Sumo wrestlers was O-nami, a name that means, literally, "Great Waves."

In practice, O-nami was so skillful that even his *sensei* was no match for him. But as soon as he entered the arena for a real match, even his own students could toss him about.

On the advice of one of the older wrestlers, O-nami went to the temple of the Zen master, Hakuju, for advice.

Hakuju told him, "Your body and spirit are not in accord. Stay in this temple all night tonight. Sit in *zazen* facing the wall, and no matter how difficult it seems, concentrate on one thing and one thing only: imagine that you are the great waves your name implies. See yourself as huge waves, strong and flowing. When you can see those waves inundating everything in their path, your problem will be solved."

With great difficulty and pain in his legs, O-nami did exactly as the Zen master had directed him. He sat until he could see himself as the waves, rushing into the shore, sweeping away trees, houses, people, and finally, the temple itself.

In the morning, Hakuju told him, "As long as you are the great waves, nothing will be able to stand in your path."

After this incident, O-nami was never again defeated.

The First Principle

More than 200 years ago, the Zen master, Kosen, wrote the calligraphy for "The First Principle" on a large scroll. This scroll was used by carpenters to trace the characters on a large piece of wood, which was then etched and draped over the gate of the Obaku temple in Kyoto. This plaque still hangs over the temple gate today, and is often referred to by modern calligraphers as "the great masterpiece."

When Kosen was working on the original calligraphy, one of his senior students, an auda-

cious lad who thought more of himself than others, happened to pass by. Examining Kosen's work, he boldly proclaimed it "terrible" and "unfit as a pattern for a plaque."

Somewhat irritated by the criticism, Kosen tried again.

"Awful," said the student. "The first one was better."

In a controlled rage, Kosen proceeded to produce character after character, until more than 80 large sheets of paper lay scattered about, none of which was good enough to receive the approval of the student.

Driven to the brink of distraction by the young man's impertinence, Kosen's calligraphy began to look amateurish.

"I can't take it any more," sighed the student. "I'm going out for a drink of water, and then I'll be back."

"Now's my chance," thought Kosen. "I'll do this calligraphy without that young smart-aleck's approval!" Turning to the paper, Kosen dipped his brush in the ink, and with a mind completely free from the distraction of his pupil, he quickly wrote, "The First Principle."

Just then the student returned. Looking at the calligraphy, he bowed deeply to Kosen, saying, "That is a great masterpiece!"

Heaven and Hell

A samurai named Nobushige asked for an audience with the Zen master, Hakuin, and asked the master, "What is Heaven and what is Hell?"

"You couldn't possibly be a samurai," replied Hakuin. "A true warrior wouldn't ask such a stupid question. Only a blockhead or a jackass would waste my time with such nonsense!"

So enraged was Nobushige by this that he began chasing Hakuin around the room, shouting that he was going to beat him senseless.

"Beat me up?" cried Hakuin. "I knew it! You're probably a beggar in disguise who doesn't even know how to use a sword!"

The furious warrior instantly drew his sword, and Hakuin shouted, "That is Hell!"

The samurai hesitated.

"That is Heaven!" said Hakuin.

Temper

One of Bankei's pupils asked the master, "*Sensei*, I have a violent, uncontrollable temper. What can I do to control it?"

"Well," said Bankei, "Show it to me."

"I can't show it to you right now," said the student.

"Okay," replied the master, "When can you show it to me."

"That's just it," said the student. "It comes and goes without warning. I can't control it."

"Hmm," said Bankei, "You say you have something but can't show it to me. If it were part of your true self, you could show it to me anytime. So, it must not be a part of your true nature, which means you didn't have it when you were born, and no one gave it to you. Think about it."

True Mastery

Zenkai, a samurai retained by a high official in Edo, was caught in the act of adultery with the official's wife. Rather than submit to punishment, Zenkai killed the official and ran away into the country with the man's wife.

Later, disillusioned by the woman's greed and pettiness, he left her and became a *ronin* (masterless warrior) in the far-away province of Buzen.

Realizing that he had thrown away his life without doing anything good, Zenkai determined that he would pay penance in the form of hard work. There was a mountain in Buzen that had a very dangerous trail over it, and many people had been killed there when the path gave way and when landslides occurred. Zenkai determined that he would dig a tunnel through the mountain for the benefit of all the people in the province.

For 30 years, Zenkai became a beggar and worked all night, every night, digging the tunnel.

In the 28th year of his labor, he was discovered by the son of the official he had killed. The son challenged him to a duel and announced that he was going to kill Zenkai to avenge his father's unjust death.

"You certainly have a right to kill me," said Zenkai, "but please consider the plight of all the people in this province. Let me finish the tunnel, and then I will gladly give you my life."

The vengeful son agreed to this, and sat down to wait. After a few months, the son grew impatient and began helping Zenkai with the tunnel. The sooner the tunnel was completed, the sooner he would be able to kill the man.

Day after day, the young man helped Zenkai dig the tunnel, and after about a year of continuous work, he came to admire Zenkai's willpower and fortitude.

When the tunnel was finally completed, it was 2,280 feet long, 20 feet high, and 30 feet wide.

"My work is finished, and my soul is free," said Zenkai. "Kill me now."

But as the young man raised his sword to cut off Zenkai's head, he suddenly started crying. Putting his sword back in the scabbard, he said, "How can I kill my own master?"

Spirit First, Techniques Second

Matajuro Yagyu was born to a very famous samurai family of swordsmen. By the time he was in his 20s, it had become painfully clear that he had no talent for swordsmanship, and his father cast him out of the house.

In spite of his father's attitude, Matajuro knew that his father was very old and would soon need support and attention. Determined to gain his father's respect, Matajuro went to the famous swordsman, Banzo, and asked to be accepted as his pupil. Banzo watched Matajuro's kata and told him, "Your father is right; you have no talent at all."

"But if I really work hard at it," said Matajuro, "how long would it take me to be proficient?"

"It would take the rest of your life," answered Banzo, "no matter how long you lived."

"But suppose I become your dedicated servant and train every day. How long would it take then?" persisted Matajuro.

"Well, under those conditions, maybe you could make it in 10 years," said Banzo.

"Good," said Matajuro, "but my father is very old, and I must become a master quickly, before he dies. How long will it take me if I train all day, every day?"

"Under those conditions," replied Banzo, "it would take at least 30 years."

"I don't understand this at all!" cried Matajuro. "First it's 10 years, and now it's 30 years! I will do anything to become a master!"

"All right," said Banzo, "but impatience is a great roadblock on the path to mastery. With your impatience, it will take you at least 75 years to master the art. I will accept you as a servant and student only if you can display patience and a calm and steady spirit, no matter what I tell you to do, and no matter what happens."

Matajuro agreed, and he moved in with Banzo the next day. "You will live by two rules," Banzo told him, "and if you violate either one, you will be expelled instantly. First, you must do exactly what I say, no matter what you think of it. Second, you are forbidden to touch a sword or speak of swordsmanship."

For three years, Matajuro cleaned the master's house, made his bed, cooked meals, washed dishes, tended the garden, and mended clothes. Then, one day while he was washing dishes and feeling sorry that he had ever entered Banzo's house, he received a terrible blow across the shoulders. Banzo had sneaked up behind him and whacked him with a wooden sword. The next day, Matajuro was tending the garden when Banzo jumped out of the bushes with a shout and whacked him hard on the back of the thighs. Day after day, and night after night, even when Matajuro was sleeping, Banzo attacked him unexpectedly. Eventually, Matajuro could think of nothing else. He still performed his mundane tasks, but his mind was filled only with the thought of Banzo's sword.

After a year of lumps and bruises, Matajuro become so aware of his surroundings that he was able to evade Banzo's surprise attacks, even when he was asleep.

Shortly thereafter, Matajuro was universally recognized as the greatest swordsman in Japan.

The Secret of Swordsmanship

Yagyu Tajima no kami Munenori was a famous swordsman who was retained as a teacher by the Shogun, Tokugawa Iyemitsu.

One day, one of the Shogun's guards approached Yagyu and asked to be accepted as a student of the sword.

"I would be happy to teach you," Yagyu said, "but it is obvious to my trained eye that you are already a master. To which *ryu* do you belong?"

"*Sensei*," replied the guard, "it shames me to tell you that I know nothing of swordsmanship. I have never studied the art."

"Don't try to make a fool of me!" roared Yagyu. "I know a master when I see one, and you have obviously studied long and hard."

"Sir," said the guard, "I am sorry to upset you, but I swear that I know nothing."

"All right," Yagyu conceded, "but the way you move tells me that you are a great master of something, and you must tell me what it is."

"Well," replied the guard, "since I was born a samurai, I knew that eventually I would have to be trained for warfare, and at a very early age I determined to practice Zen to overcome my fear of death. After many years of practice and meditation, I can honestly say that I have solved the problem, and death holds no meaning for me. Perhaps this is what you are sensing."

"That's it!" cried Yagyu. "I was right. Of all the hundreds of students I have trained in the way of the sword, not one of them has yet received a certificate of mastery from me, because they are all still afraid of dying. You, however, have practiced Zen until you have completely transcended matters of life and death."

"You need no technical training. You are already a great master."

What You See is What You Believe

It is said that a young prince lived with his father in a palace on the shores of the ocean. The prince led an idyllic life and daily strolled along his private beach to gaze out over the water and watch the birds flying gently in the breeze. One day he was startled to suddenly see a large island appear with dragons and monsters cavorting and fighting all over it. As he jumped back, he was again startled by a voice behind him that roared, "What's the matter?" Turning, the frightened boy beheld a fierce-looking man wearing a black evening coat with large sleeves.

"Who are you and where did that island and those monsters come from?" the prince stammered.

"Why, I created them and put them there!" laughed the man.

"Then you must be God!" the prince cried.

"Of course I'm God!" came the fierce reply.

Terrified, the prince ran home and blurted the whole story to his father.

"This man you saw," replied the father calmly, "was he wearing a black evening coat with large sleeves?"

"Yes," answered the prince, "but what has that to do with anything?"

"The man you saw was not God," replied the father. "He was a magician. All magicians wear black evening coats with large sleeves. I am a magician, too, and he is my friend. Now, for the first time, you notice that I also wear such an evening coat. I asked my friend to create an illusion and frighten you so that you could become a man and see things as they really are. You have lived in illusion long enough. There is no island, there are no monsters, and you are not a prince. We are common people, and it is time for you to know that. I created illusions for your happiness as a child. Go and see for yourself."

After seeing that what his father had told him was indeed true, the boy returned home, where his father was drinking tea with his friend.

"Father," said the boy, "you were right, but I cannot accept this. If I can't be a prince, I would rather be dead."

"Fine," replied the father, beckoning his son to kneel before him. "My friend will now kill you."

The boy thought it was a joke until he saw the very real blade of the friend's sword descending upon him.

"Wait!" he cried. "I understand!" Whereupon the three men wordlessly had a cup of tea and went out to tend their fields.

Perspective

The Zen master, Tokai, was sleeping one night when a fire broke out in the kitchen of the temple. A pupil rushed into Tokai's room, screaming, "Fire, *Sensei*! Fire!"

"Fire?" said Tokai. "Where?"

"In the kitchen, *Sensei*! You must get up! The monks are trying to put it out!"

"Well," said Tokai, yawning, "the kitchen is on the other side of the temple. If the fire reaches my hallway, you be sure and wake me up again, okay? Good night."

So saying, Tokai lay down and slept soundly.

Do What Must be Done

In about his 75th year, the Zen master, Goyu, was told by his doctor that he needed surgery on his eye. Goyu told the doctor to do what must be done.

Anesthesia was not a highly developed science at that time, and was usually reserved for the very old, to help them stand the pain. On the day of the operation, the doctor explained the anesthesia to Goyu, who said, "I do not need that; just do what must be done."

Throughout the operation, Goyu sat calmly, unflinching, in a straight-backed chair.

The doctor said it appeared as if Goyu were somewhere else.

You Cannot Attack Emptiness

It is said that a young monk inadvertently insulted a great samurai. Although the monk could not understand what he had done wrong, he immediately sought to apologize. The samurai, being a braggart and one full of self-pride and vanity, rejected the apology and demanded satisfaction. No matter how hard he tried, the monk could not dissuade the warrior from his foolish position. Being of a lower caste in society, the monk was obliged to obey the ruffian's demands, and agreed to meet him at dawn for a duel to the death. As was the custom, the warrior gave the monk a sword and sent him away to prepare for the battle.

The monk, having no knowledge of swordsmanship or fighting, was sure that he would lose his life, and went to the master of his monastery for advice.

"Your mind is too full of fear and thoughts about what will happen," said the priest. "Sit in solitary meditation all night, with the sword raised above your head, as if prepared to strike. Close your eyes and meditate only on the sensation of 'cool.' When blade meets flesh, the sensation is one of thin and cool. Clear your mind completely. Empty it, and then fill it with one purpose only: When you feel something cool, strike down with the sword."

Though perplexed at first, the monk obeyed his master. Throughout the night he held the sword above his head and meditated on the one thought only, until everything else left his mind.

When he met the loudmouth the next morning, he bowed, raised the sword above his head, and closed his eyes. His fear was gone, and he waited to feel the sensation of cool steel.

"Fight, coward!" cried the samurai. "Open your eyes and fight!"

But the monk made no response. He heard nothing and saw nothing. His only purpose was to make his one strike.

It is said that the samurai, after a long period of intense silence, sheathed his sword, bowed humbly in defeat, and walked away.

It is impossible to attack emptiness.

Fate

The great and famous warrior, Nobunaga, once faced the prospect of going into battle with his men outnumbered 10 to one. The men were scared, but Nobunaga was confident that if they could launch a surprise attack before sunrise, they could win.

So he told his men that while he was confident they would win, he would leave it to

the Gods. He would offer a prayer, he said, in a Shinto shrine and ask the Gods to reveal to him the fate of him and his troops.

The soldiers waited restlessly while Nobunaga prayed, and when he came out, he said he had been instructed to flip a coin. If the coin came up heads, fate would be on their side. If it came up tails, they would perish.

When he flipped the coin and heads appeared, his men were ecstatic. The next day, they attacked and easily defeated the enemy.

Nobunaga's attendant, surveying the carnage on the battlefield, said, "I can't believe this. I will never again doubt the hand of fate in the affairs of men."

"Me either," said Nobunaga, flipping him a two-headed coin. "Me either."

An Enlightened Man

A disciple once asked a Zen master of old if he was familiar with the Christian Bible.

"No," replied the master. "Read it to me."

The disciple read, "And why take ye thought for raiment? Consider the lilies of the field, how they grow. They toil not, neither do they spin, and yet I say unto you that even Solomon in all his glory was not arrayed like one of these.... Take therefore no thought for the morrow, for the morrow shall take thought for the things of itself."

Said the master, "Whoever said that is an enlightened man."

Delicious

One day, a monk out for a walk was suddenly threatened by a tiger, and he ran as fast as he could to escape. The tiger chased him to the edge of a cliff, and the man jumped, catching on to a vine, and ended up suspended in mid-air.

Looking down, he saw another tiger jumping up and snapping at his heels.

Looking back up, he saw two mice gnawing at the vine.

Just then, he noticed a wild berry growing on another vine within arm's reach.

He plucked the berry, took a bite of it, and said, "How delicious!"

A Whack on the Head

A monk who had studied with his master for many years, decided he wanted to visit some other monasteries to compare what they taught. When he suggested this to the master, the master picked up a stick and whacked him on the head.

The monk asked several more times, but every time he got a whack on the head.

Finally, in exasperation, he went to a much older monk and asked him to intercede for him. This the old monk did and reported back to the young man that it was all set up. "The master has agreed to hear your request," he informed the young man.

However, when the young monk kept his appointment and asked the master for permission, the master simply whacked him on the head again.

"I can't believe it," said the older monk. "The master always keeps his word. I'll ask him about it."

He went to the master and asked him why he had withdrawn his permission after saying he would grant it.

"I didn't change my mind," said the master. "I simply wanted to give him a last whack on the head because when he comes back from his journey, he'll be enlightened, and I won't be able to hit him anymore."

* * * * *

A Real Teacher

"If you feel that the teacher is a real teacher,
  Then give up your own ideas, and learn."
  — First verse of the *Hundred Verses of the Spear*.

PEN

What is Karate?

The art of karate (literally, "empty hands") is a method of unarmed combat that was developed and systematized by the Okinawan people, beginning about 1600 A.D. The Okinawans were forbidden (first by their own rulers and later by their Japanese conquerors) to possess weapons. Under several successive bans, the Okinawans were even forced to check out farming implements in the morning and return them before sundown. Since armed samurai were prone to attack Okinawan peasants on whim, the Okinawans were forced to rely on their wits and their bare hands for survival. They learned fighting techniques from Chinese seamen and gradually combined these with their own, indigenous techniques to form a system of combat that came to be known as *te* or Okinawa-te (meaning "hands"). Over the centuries, Okinawa-te became highly developed, and tales of the exploits of its practitioners spread far into both China and Japan.

As Okinawa-te developed and gained more practitioners, it split into several distinctive styles (*ryu*), each reflecting the stylistic preferences of various masters in different villages. Several of these styles continued to be practiced as the Okinawan people gained their freedom and moved into the 20th century.

By 1905, the art was considered benign enough to be demonstrated in public. The first public exhibition was given by Gichin Funakoshi (1868–1957), a school teacher and poet who was widely known by his pen name, "Shoto."

In 1917, Funakoshi traveled to Japan to demonstrate his art to a few Japanese, and returned to Japan again in 1922 at the official invitation of the Japanese Ministry of Education. The Okinawan masters chose Funakoshi to represent them in Japan primarily because of his fluency in the Japanese language. Further, Funakoshi was the best educated, most highly refined, and cultured man among the Okinawan martial artists of that time. He was also the highly respected president of the Okinawan Martial Spirit Promotion Society.

Funakoshi was invited to formally introduce his art to the Japanese at their National Sports Exhibition, an annual event attended by the Royal Family. Being an extremely humble and sincere man, Funakoshi desired to represent all of Okinawan karate to the Japanese rather than just his own, favored style. Accordingly, he visited each Okinawan master of repute and asked each one to teach him the techniques that best represented the individual school. These techniques he took to Japan in the form of 15 kata, a kata being a formal exercise routine composed of from 15 to 65 techniques of blocking, punching, striking, and kicking.

The art already was called karate by 1922, the ideogram for "kara" meaning "Chinese" and referring to the T'ang dynasty. Funakoshi never returned to Okinawa, and he later changed the character for "kara" to one drawn from the Zen Buddhist tradition, meaning "empty" or "rendering oneself empty." Thus it is that today when we say "karate," we are speaking of a purely Japanese art that conforms, in spirit and essence, to the traditional Japanese precepts of chivalry, duty, honor, and so on.

There are many different karate *ryu* in Japan and Okinawa today, but the largest school is still Funakoshi's school—the

Shotokan school. "Kan" means "building," and Shoto was Funakoshi's pen name. Thus, Shotokan karate-do is the "way of the empty hand taught at Shoto's building," and it has become a recognized part of the body of techniques and arts known as Japanese martial arts or martial ways (*budo*).

Japanese martial arts are unique in that most of them purport to be sporting activities, but at the same time claim that sport is only a very small part of the overall discipline. Indeed, many martial arts, such as iaido (way of the live blade) and aikido (way of spirit harmony) have no sporting aspects at all. In most sports (hockey, baseball, football, and so on), the rule is the sport. Without official rules, there would be no hockey, no baseball, no football, and so on. We refer to such sports as "pure" sports because they are complete within themselves. They have no significant application to any sphere of existence larger than themselves.

"Japanese martial arts...claim that sport is only a very small part of the overall discipline."

For the most part, however, physical training in martial arts like karate consists of formalized methods for logically studying and practicing natural and necessary body movements — "natural" in that the movements are derived from intuitive response to surprise attack, and "necessary" in that the movements were born of the survival instinct. All martial arts with sporting rules would continue to function quite well with the elimination of those rules. And all "pure" martial arts bear direct applications to the larger spheres of day-to-day life, personality, psychological stability, and survival.

We say that karate-do is pure *budo* because it conforms, in spirit and essence, to the traditional precepts of *budo*. The word, *budo*, is derived from Chinese characters that are combinations of other characters. "*Bu*" is a combination of two characters, one meaning "halberd" or "sword," and the other meaning "to stop." *Do* means "way" or "path." Thus, *budo* means "to stop conflict" or "the way that promotes peace."

The philosophy of *budo* is opposed to conflict. In karate-do we strive to develop enough power to control any dangerous situation and thereby promote peace. And far more power is required to control a situation than simply to win a fight. This is similar to the deterrent theory of international politics: Let your enemies know that you have tremendous power and confidence, and they will be less likely to attack you.

In *budo*, however, we do not menace or threaten the opponent, but simply control the situation on whatever level it develops. In this way, the opponent will get the idea quickly, and the cause of peace will be advanced. With these principles in mind, the informed practitioner will not view karate or other martial arts purely as sports.

In karate, the spirit of actual fighting (*jissen*) is thought of in terms of fire. There is nothing to fear from a fire that is contained and controlled; without fuel, it will burn itself out. The goal of the karateka (practitioner of karate) under attack is to contain and control the attacker. Rarely is it necessary to destroy the opponent.

We call karate-do an art because it presupposes unique abilities in each human being, but does not encourage the development of these abilities for the purpose of competition with others. Karate-do seeks to maximize strengths and minimize weaknesses for the benefit of the individual alone. There is no game to win and no important match to lose. There is only the individual striving to bring their being into concert with the laws of nature and into harmony with the ebb and flow of humanity.

To defeat an opponent is not the final purpose of karate training in its modern manifestation. The ultimate aim of karate is development of the character of those who practice it, and rigorous discipline is required to attain that goal. Students must learn to defend themselves unarmed, using various parts of the body for blocking, punching, striking, and kicking.

> "Karate-do seeks to maximize strengths and minimize weaknesses for the benefit of the individual alone."

Besides being a superior form of self-defense, karate also is an ideal physical art, making balanced use of all parts of the body.

Because karate has proven to be such an effective form of self-defense, it has grown rapidly in popularity throughout the world in recent years.

Additionally, the sport aspect of karate has increased greatly in popularity. The beauty of the form and the speed and excitement of karate matches draws more and more spectators to karate tournaments every year.

As physical conditioning, karate is unsurpassed in the development of coordination, agility, endurance, and strength, and the training can be adapted to every individual, regardless of age, sex, or physique. Anyone who can participate in regular, moderate physical activity can learn karate.

Ironically, strength and athletic ability are of little importance in the practice of karate. What is important is the balanced use of the entire body and mind. Technique without the unification of mind and body, spirit and will, will fail in time of crisis. And this unification of mind and action must become a part of the nature of the practitioner—not only in combat, but in every phase of daily life.

The art of karate must be studied with humility and sincerity. Students who persevere will gain confidence, gentleness, and self-control. Through rigorous training of the mind and body and overcoming problems and stress situations placed before them by their teacher, students gain strength and confidence in themselves, both physically and mentally. Fears disappear, and students are able to relate to others without antagonism or feelings of inferiority. Because of their newly found strength, students of karate tend to find the problems of everyday living less ominous. When they become confident that they can meet all others on an equal level without fear, karate students tend to be less perplexed by problematic situations.

Karate teaches that the mind must be clear and objective, like the clear, undisturbed surface of a pond, which reflects all things surrounding it equally and exactly as they are. If the water is in tumult, it cannot reflect clearly. So it is with the mind. If the mind is disturbed and muddled, it cannot reflect objectively on the situation at hand, and the proper course of action is left to chance.

A clear, reflective mind is cultivated through strictly disciplined concentration upon the intentions, techniques, and movements of one's adversary. In the dojo, a lapse in total concentration means instant defeat. In actual combat, the results could be disastrous.

In the dojo, students must commit 100 percent of their attention to the intentions and movements of the opponent, and once the attack is perceived, act instantly to re-direct it against itself. In time, students carry with them from the dojo this sense of awareness, concentration, and confidence.

It is common to hear that the best defense is a good offense, but one who is proficient in karate knows that the best defense is avoidance of any situation that may lead to conflict. If avoidance is not possible, running away and seeking shelter is the best course of action. Students who train with commitment and humility learn to run with confidence.

However, if a surprise attack occurs suddenly without warning, and if all possible courses of reason and escape have been exhausted, karate students are taught to act instantly, with utter commitment to protecting themselves.

As a method of self-defense, karate is completely functional for healthy people of all ages. The physical techniques are fast, powerful, and completely effective in any situation requiring self-defense.

Technique (*Jutsu*) and Art (*Do*)

In almost all serious activities, there is an apparent difference between technique (*jutsu*) and art (*do*). All painters, for example, know the proper way to hold a pallet, ink the brush, and stretch canvas. They know the particular techniques of protecting and preserving canvas until the paint dries. These are somewhat mechanical techniques that can be learned by almost anyone who has the desire to learn them. Certain judgment is required to make the correct adjustments in the canvas, to mix just the right consistency in the paints, and so on, but there is nothing inherently artistic in the skill to make such judgments: it is a skill acquired through experience.

The difference between artists and skillful technicians is that no matter how hard they try, technicians cannot create great works of art. Technicians, through skilled technique, paint pictures; artists, through the force and drive of their spirit, create works of art.

We do not know why some people possess creative talent and some do not, but we do know that most people possess at least some modicum of talent that does not surface without stimulation. That is, most people at one time or another feel an urge to draw, paint, or write, but find it impossible to do so because of their circumstances. Some coaching is necessary, and most people never get it.

In this regard, karate-do is unique. The purpose of karate-do is to help individuals realize their own potential and expand the limits of their capabilities in all areas of life.

The purpose of karate-do is not to learn a particular thing or perform a particular technique. The purpose is to explore our own abilities and talents, to understand them in the light of reality, and to use them. This is why karate-do is truly a martial art—an art of understanding ourselves. And it is a true art form that is available to everyone without regard to or restriction from age, sex, race, education, social status, religious belief, or philosophy.

The *do* of karate-do, then, is a universal method of developing awareness of ourselves, our talents, our hidden or unused abilities, our environment, and the purposes and intentions of others. The techniques of karate-do are the method we use to confront ourselves, facing mental and physical obstacles and striving to understand and become more aware of the functions of our bodies and minds. The actualization of karate-do is a piercing awareness of both ourselves and all that is relevant in the external environment. Once this actualization is realized, we are able to move through life like an artist—perceiving the world and expressing ourselves through the force and drive of our spirit.

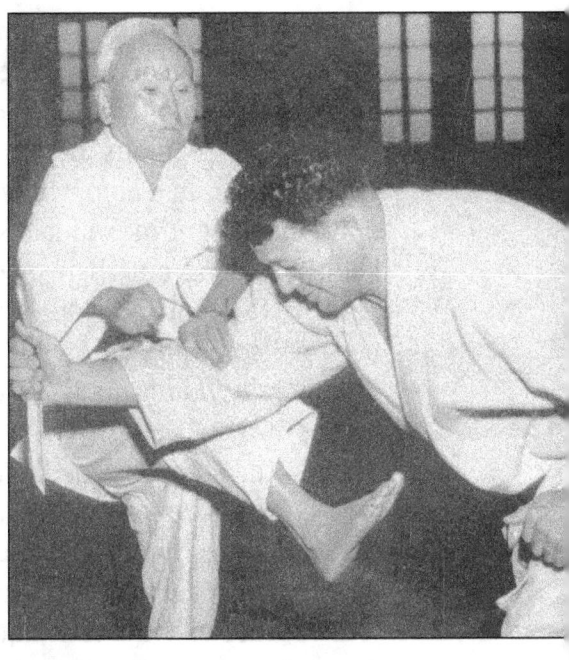

"The do of karate-do, then, is a universal method of developing awareness."

The realization of karate-do can be attained in only one way: the mind must be emptied of all its impressions, ideas, and illusions. It must be cleared completely and made receptive to feeling and intuition. This is a very difficult, life-long task.

From the moment we are born, and perhaps in the womb, we form impressions and concepts of ourselves and the world around us. But these impressions often are faulty. If we are raised in affluence, we cannot truly understand poverty; if raised in poverty and hunger, we can only guess at the virtues and benefits of wealth. The importance of the truly aware mind is that it can enable us to feel and understand the universal feelings of humanity. In the *dojo* there are no rich and poor, no famous and infamous, no favored and discarded, and no differences in race. In a *dojo* where true karate-do is taught, there is only one action: individuals striving to unite their minds and bodies, seeking out their own strengths and weaknesses, and relating to other individuals as peers in a cooperative spirit of personal communication and common desire.

Literally, *do* means "way" or "path." Thus karate-do literally means "way of the empty hand," with the emphasis on "way." That is, the study of true karate-do is a continuous journey on a path. Mastery of the art is not accomplished with mere mastery of the techniques. Rather, mastery of karate-do is a life-long journey along a path toward perfection of character—a journey that uses the techniques and training as the vehicle for progress along that path.

> *"Mastery of karate-do is a life-long journey along a path toward perfection of character."*

Therefore, it must be remembered that the "doing" of karate on a daily basis is the essence of the art. Setting long-range goals for one's progress in the techniques is useless. The only worthy goal is to resolve to make yourself better today than you were yesterday and to seek harmony with yourself, other people, and the world around you.

Psychological Principles

Essentially, psychological well being is strive for in karate-do through harmonizing the functions of the body with those of the mind. This is accomplished through arduous physical training with strong emphasis on discipline.

The mind and body must function as one.

Students of the art may find help in achieving this harmony by studying certain basic concepts and trying to relate these concepts to their training and daily lives.

Following are the most basic concepts of karate-do psychology.

A Mind Like Water
Mizu no Kokoro

Consider the water in a pond or forest lake. If the water is calm and clear, it will reflect everything around it, like a finely polished mirror. If the water is in tumult, the reflections will be distorted.

In karate training, we should strive to imagine our minds as the calm surface of that pond, seeing everything around us exactly as everything is. As the pond reflects everything around its entire circumference, so should our minds try to reflect everything in a circle around us. In this way, the mind can clearly perceive everything that is relevant in the external environment—even the most minute movements of the opponent.

If any thought is allowed to enter the mind, the effect will be that of casting a stone in the water. The clear surface will be distorted and the reflections altered. The movements of the opponent will not be clear, and the proper response will be left to chance.

A Mind Like the Moon
Tsuki no Kokoro

Overlooking the clear pond of the mind should be the moon.

The light of the moon is different from the light of the sun. While the sun shines brightly and casts harsh shadows, the moon shines more evenly and gently. Harsh shadows conceal, while softer shadows do not hide completely. Further, the moon shines down equally on all below it, without the sharp angles of the sun.

A mind like the moon in karate means that you should see the opponent's whole body as equally as possible. Seeing only one part of the opponent's body will cause one to lose sight of the rest, and defeat is inevitable.

One-Punch Death-Blow
Ikken Hisatsu

In order to look deeply into your own nature, you must practice with the idea that each movement balances between life and death and that there is never a second chance. To accomplish this, practice with the intention of making every technique a one-punch death-blow. That is, every block, punch, kick, and strike should be practiced with such intensity that it can disable an opponent with only one impact. Of course, modern karate training has no intention of killing anyone, but this level of seriousness is necessary to master the techniques and delve deeply into human nature.

Offense and Defense are One
Kobo Itchi

If you think that punching, kicking, and striking are offensive and that blocking is defensive, you will never penetrate the deeper meanings of the techniques or your own nature. Remember that the "doing" of karate techniques is more important than theorizing about them—more important, even, than the outcome of them. This maxim is an admonition to just practice without theorizing or thinking about the techniques. Practice until every technique, in and of itself, is an effective offense and defense.

Mind and Technique are One
Shingi Ittai

If your mind is "fixed" anywhere or is in turmoil or is concentrating on anything or is thinking or is responding to fear, it will be reflected in your technique. Any thought entering the mind causes a pause, which is reflected both in your response to an attack and in your technique.

It is extremely important to learn to empty the mind completely and to respond to any threat naturally, from the center of your body, mind, and spirit.

Everyday Mind
Heijo Shin

This means that you should strive to develop a calm, steadfast state of mind that remains the same whether you are going about your daily business, training in the dojo, or facing a real attack.

If your mind is empty of fears, illusions, and confusion, you will be able to respond instantly and naturally in any situation. Otherwise, whatever is in your mind will have to be cleared away before you can respond, and that extra time may mean the difference between life and death.

One Mind—Remaining Mind
Isshin-Zanshin

Isshin means "one mind," and *zanshin* means "remaining mind." *Zanshin* is a mind like the ocean—aware, active, and generally in motion. *Isshin* is a mind like the wave—it has one

purpose and direction only, and it sweeps away all that is in its path.

The idea is to keep your mind always alive, alert, and aware (like the ocean) and to let *isshin* manifest itself when you perform a technique, returning instantly to *zanshin*.

The most important thing, though, is to cultivate the state of *zanshin* (the ocean) because *isshin* (the wave) is contained in it.

Both the Eyes and the Mind Must See
Kan-Ken Futatsu No Koto

Ken is the eyes seeing the surface of things—seeing what is actually illuminated by light. *Kan* is the mind penetrating through the surface of things and perceiving their true nature. Anyone can look at an opponent, for example, and see what the opponent is doing, but karate-do training enables you to see beyond what is evident with the eyes. With proper training, you can perceive the nature and intentions of your opponent, and in many cases respond to an attack before it even physically occurs.

Osu

Osu is a contraction of *osae* (meaning "to press") and *shinobu* (meaning "patience" or "steady spirit"). *Osu* is what karate students say when they greet each other, depart from each other, attack each other, and indicate that they are ready to receive an attack. It is also used as an affirmative reply to questions in the *dojo*, but it does not always mean "yes." When the *sensei* asks you if you understand a particular thing, and you reply, "*Osu!*", what you are saying is that, even if you don't fully understand it, you are willing to keep or press your patience—that your spirit is satisfied until you can understand it better.

It is similar to the idea of two people riding in a car on an icy road on the edge of a deep canyon. If you are the passenger, and the driver says, "Are you okay?", you might reply, "*Osu!*", indicating that while there is nothing you can do to make the situation better or less dangerous at the moment, your spirit is satisfied that the best that can be done at the moment is being done. You are telling the driver that you will calmly and steadfastly keep patience during this difficult time. When you enter the *dojo* and say, "*Osu!*", you are announcing to all present that you have brought your patient and steady spirit with you and that you are in the *dojo* to do your best.

Kinesthesia

The kinesthetic sense is the movement sense. By definition it is "the sense whose end organs lie in the muscles, tendons, and joints and are stimulated by bodily tensions; the muscle sense."

The movement sense is the sense that informs us of muscular events that occur in our own body. The kinesthetic sense works in conjunction with the semi-circular canals in the ear, which tell us about balance, posture, and position. Thus, we know whether we are upside down or right side up. Even with our eyes closed, we can be aware of movement, because sense organs that respond to movement (just as the organs of sight respond to light) are embedded in the tissue of the muscles and in the tendons and joints.

As the eye receives a rich variety of impressions through light waves that stimulate the visual receptors in terms of light, shadow, color, hue, and intensity, so we experience a wide variety of impressions through our kinesthetic sense. We are able to perceive the position of our body and the relationship of its parts. We can feel different states of tension and release in our own muscles. Through the kinesthetic sense we are aware of the velocity of our movements.

Each sense has corresponding art forms that employ the materials of that sense for their media. The auditory sense has a corresponding art form—music—whose medium is sound. Similarly, the kinesthetic sense has a corresponding art form—karate—that uses the medium of movement.

In any art form, the learning of a technique centers around gaining mastery of the instrument and the medium. In music one is trained to control the instrument to produce subtle variations of sound. One studies the properties of sound. In music one trains the ear to learn to hear in a highly sensitive manner.

In karate, the body is the instrument, and movement is the medium. It should be understood then, that karate training centers around gaining a mastery over the body and its movements. Since motion is our medium, we should concern ourselves with the elements of motion: space, time, and energy. Learning karate technique is learning to feel kinesthetically in a highly sensitive manner.

We usually tend to feel movement superficially. The sensations usually are indefinite. As we work kinesthetically with movement, as opposed to visually before a mirror, the muscular sensations become more definite and conscious. The more definite the perception, the greater is the depth of learning, and the more deeply the movement becomes imbedded in our motor memories. Subtle variations in quality and shape become apparent. The vague, indefinite mass of movement becomes an intricate spectrum of motion through kinesthetic training.

> *"In karate, the body is the instrument, and movement is the medium."*

One of the purposes of karate training is, through discipline, to teach the body to move spontaneously with great skill. To come to this point requires a strong grasp on the nature of the human body and motion, and an understanding of movement concepts provides a factual basis for this development. By studying motion as a vital element of inner and outer functioning, we extend our knowledge of ourselves and our media. By pursuing this knowledge and seeking heightened kinesthetic awareness, we can approach mastery of karate.

If we view the gaining of technique as an enlarging of our expressive means, then a technique class is an opportunity to concentrate on movement, perceive it, assimilate it, and live it.

Movement is the main material of karate. In developing and mastering its spiritual and emotional values as well as its organic functions, you build up your own body, so that it becomes what it should be: the ideal instrument of the art of motion.

Students coming into karate class for the first time usually do not know they have a kinesthetic sense. Both intellectually and sensorially, they are unaware of the sense of motion.

Learning karate is a constant challenge to feel what is going on in your own body. The most difficult thing to understand is that the development of karate technique is completely a matter of self-discipline. Your own kinesthetic sense must be trained, and this is achieved only through constant practice and introspective effort.

Kata is the most valuable tool for working with the elements of movement, time, space, and energy, and it helps you gain an understanding of fundamental principles that can be used in any movement situation, so that the experience gained in *kata* practice can illuminate every other movement situation.

A karate class is an opportunity to use your body and mind creatively, and practicing karate should always involve strong physical, mental, and emotional concentration.

Karate and Physical Fitness

Today people in virtually every industrialized society are participating vigorously in various forms of physical fitness activities. This is particularly true in America, where the boom in tennis, racquetball, handball, aerobics, and jogging has been going on for many years, and shows no signs of abating. Large corporations invest millions of dollars in the development of health and fitness facilities. And while increased concern for physical fitness is good for both the individual and society in general, it could be, through an art like karate-do, a whole lot more.

The benefits of karate training over other forms of exercise may best be seen from a historical perspective of physical education. While none of us was present at the dawn of humanity, we can assume that it was a very difficult time in which to live. As humans struggled for survival against the elements and other creatures, they knew intuitively that the strong live longer than the weak. While this may not necessarily be true today, it was certainly true then. Survival of the fittest was a very cold reality. It is difficult and even absurd to envision a cave dweller doing push-ups and jogging, but we can readily accept that such people were, by our standards, inordinately strong. We know, for example, that primitive people often ran for miles, chasing an animal into exhaustion for the purpose of killing and eating it. And we know that while a horse is lucky to travel 40 miles in one day, the Apache Indians in 19th century America frequently covered two or three times that distance on foot to avoid the U.S. Cavalry. When there were no machines to do the hard labor, muscle power was a very valuable commodity. The physical education of primitive people was not based on rules or organized sports; it was a natural by-product of their natural and necessary activities.

As we have progressed and industrialized, our reliance on fitness for survival has diminished drastically. Today we have machines to do everything. More machines and more technology require more education and intellectual development. While the level of literacy and higher education generally reflects the level of "civilization" of a society, it is also true that people in more primitive cultures today frequently outlive their "civilized" counterparts. Many factors in modern society contribute to this, of course, such as pollution of the environment, chemicals in the food chain, ever-mutating viruses, and so on. And while it is true that our life spans are longer now than they were even five years ago, it is debatable how valuable and enjoyable those added years are in light of physical and mental debilitation. After many years of directing society along a path leading to more leisure time, people are beginning to place more emphasis on feeling good to better enjoy their leisure.

That regular vigorous exercise improves the overall functioning of the body is undisputed. However, there is scanty proof that people who exercise regularly live any longer, on the whole, than those who do not. We still are not sure, for example, whether people who exercise regularly are healthier because of the exercise, or if healthier people tend to exercise more regularly than their less healthy peers.

Why, then, all the emphasis on fitness? Because people who exercise regularly *feel* a lot better than those who don't exercise, and their mental processes function more smoothly.

Virtually all forms of physical fitness today revolve around sport or dance, not survival. While some people jog or do calisthenics daily with no thought of sport, they do so only out of a desire for fitness—not as part of an underlying philosophy. While sports share the philosophy of achieving excellence, that is as far as the philosophy carries over into daily life. Achieving excellence in a given sport does not necessarily carry positive emotional, philosophical, or mental factors into daily living.

We have all seen champion athletes who become stars and *prima donnas*, using their inflated egos to intimidate others. At the same time, we know that becoming a champion at any sport is the result of long, hard work and sacrifice. What we may infer from this is that the hard work and discipline necessary to rise to the top in sports does not necessarily develop better character. Character development is presaged by understanding oneself and one's fellow human beings, but in sport it is necessary only to understand the rules and the opponent.

The karate view is that any physical fitness is better than none, but the best physical fitness is that which arises from the natural, instinctual processes that people inherit but have forgotten how to use. Such fitness comes from re-awakening and sharpening the natural impulse for survival. When survival is the key element, the matter of sport becomes inconsequential.

> *"The best physical fitness is that which arises from the natural, instinctual processes that people inherit but have forgotten how to use."*

Thus, while pop philosophies may evolve from sports and the desire for fitness, it is better for sports and fitness to evolve from an underlying philosophy.

The philosophy of *budo* calls for the development of the whole person—physically, mentally, emotionally, spiritually, and socially. When sport becomes the main thrust of training, with emphasis on winning and losing, modesty and humility are destroyed, and the essence of *budo* is lost.

Many karate masters say that karate is a natural skill, like swimming, which humans have forgotten how to do and, like swimming, karate will always be a part of individuals once it is awakened in them. This should not be taken to mean that once a certain level of skill is reached, we may stop training. Such an attitude, although common among many Westerners, is very foolish. Any skill—including swimming—will deteriorate if not practiced regularly. A swimmer who does not practice regularly may well retain enough skill to save themselves from drowning, but little else. Similarly, the

> *"The philosophy of* budo *calls for the development of the whole person—physically, mentally, emotionally, spiritually, and socially."*

advanced karateka who stops training may retain enough survival instinct to sense danger, but may be powerless to respond appropriately. And once the training stops, the body declines more rapidly.

Again, it is very difficult to enjoy a longer life in a debilitated body.

Karate as a Point of View

Physically, karate is a method of unarmed self-defense consisting of techniques of blocking, punching, striking, and kicking. These techniques are designed for defense against surprise attacks from both armed and unarmed assailants. More than any other martial art, karate stresses defense against surprise attack, and since no weapons or special equipment are needed, it is the most practical of all the self-defense arts. Its only weapon is one's own body, a weapon that is always present. The training method is designed to increase awareness and sensitivity (ultimately eliminating the chance of surprise attack), and to develop tremendous force from relatively small movements of the body.

Of greatest importance, however, is the fact that karate is a martial art that aspires to teach us a way of life. Central to this subject is an understanding of how differently the Eastern and Occidental minds perceive their world.

In general, the Western mind takes postulation and reasoning as its basic approach to viewing the world. Once a problem or unique situation is perceived, the relevant facts are gathered and analyzed, and a decision is made. The Western world has enjoyed a higher technology and higher standard of living for a longer time than has the Asian world, and growth in technology leads to more and more reliance on science, reasoning, logic, and postulation (phenomena observed, for better or worse, more and more in modern Japan).

The basic Eastern point of view, on the other hand, is based largely on intuition or "gut feeling." This is perhaps due to lengthy societal development under more primitive conditions. For 2,000 years, Japan, for example, enjoyed a highly developed social structure without Western technology or a Renaissance or an Age of Reason. The feudal system put weapons in the hands of an elite few, and the common people were forced by circumstance to devote their mental powers to basic survival. In the face of a sword, survival is paramount, and there simply is no time for reasoning or postulating or thinking at all. Eastern religions developed accordingly, and were strongly influenced by Zen after about 600 A.D.

It is this world view—intuition over postulation—that forms the foundation of Asian martial arts and makes them so difficult for Westerners to comprehend.

Further confusion is owed to the fact that the West has tended to view nature as an entity apart from humanity—something to be conquered, subjugated, controlled and changed. The East views humanity as an integral element of nature—an element that should exist in accord with natural laws. Western ideologies tend to fight against nature from the outside; Eastern ideologies tend to encourage people to fight against themselves to create a more pleasant existence from the inside.

The karate viewpoint is that what you see, or how you view the world, is what you believe. In other words, we all live with various illusions and believe them to be true. The purpose of karate-do is to help us see things as they really are, and to broaden the scope and depth of our understanding.

The essence of karate philosophy is the breaking of attachments. This is based on the premise that people naturally feel attachments to "things," and only a greater force will make them let go. This is easily illustrated by assuming you have $100 in your pocket. Until some greater force comes to bear, you will keep the money. The greater force that makes you release it may be a robbery, a bill to pay, or simply your desire to have something that costs $100. In any case, you remain attached to it until a greater force makes you let go of it.

> *"The karate viewpoint is that what you see, or how you view the world, is what you believe."*

We live by memory and experience, and we tend to fear and avoid things that are beyond our experience. Even with strong motivation, we naturally try to retain our attachments. Everyone wants to go to heaven, for example, but no one wants to die to get there.

The purpose of karate-do is to teach us to live fearlessly—not by memory, but in the present—without attachments to anything but life itself. Without illusion or attachment, we can live life like the cherry blossom: living brilliantly with a purpose, then letting go of life all at once when the purpose is fulfilled. This is called *isagi-*

yoku: to let go of life when the time is right, without fear or regret or second thoughts.

Admittedly, this is not an easy course to follow, and that is why karate is a lifetime art. The illusions and attachments are many and ever-changing, and constant discipline is required to overcome them.

Most Westerners will accept the premise that how you view the world determines what you believe, but then would use linear logic to follow with, "What you believe is what you do, and what you do is who you are." Thus, when asked, "Who is John Smith?", we reply that he is a doctor or a carwash attendant, or whatever. And we reply in that fashion because we perceive him to be what he does. The martial art idea is that "What you believe is what you are," and what you do may be irrelevant. We therefore may decide to be karate masters because we believe it to be paramount in our lives. At the same time, we may choose to do anything else (medicine, car washing, and so on) without giving up the broadening horizons of our minds.

The distinction is subtle, but necessary to achieve the ultimate goals of karate-do.

Centering

The fundamental methods of Zen are passive, while the fundamental methods of karate are active. In Zen, the process of enlightenment usually occurs over a long period of time, which involves meditation, self-deprivation, and daily guidance from the master. In karate *dojos*, the word enlightenment is rarely, if ever, heard. In the *dojo*, the training is always active. The students are told to "move without thinking" and to "clear the mind." But these instructions are always given during physical activity, and are complemented by continuous emphasis on timing.

The ultimate timing we strive for in karate is the timing that enables us to counter-attack the opponent between the time their mind makes the decision to attack and their body actually moves to attack. In self-defense we train to perceive the attack before it occurs, and thus never be surprised. When we know an attack is imminent, we can usually escape without fighting. While this concept may sound mysterious, it really is something anyone can learn through proper training of the mind, body, and spirit.

The essence of proper timing lies in sensitivity to other people and, again using the analogy of the cherry blossom, "letting go" of attachment (in this case the attachment being thinking itself).

Thinking causes tension, and tension causes slow response. Even physically, speed is not a result of how quickly we contract the agonistic muscles, but how completely we relax the antagonistic muscles. In punching, for example, the main agonistic muscle is the triceps (the muscle that contracts to propel the arm), and the main antagonist is the biceps (the muscle that must relax to let the agonist do its work). No matter how hard we try, we cannot punch fast if the biceps is tense. Similarly, we cannot respond quickly if the mind is tense, and the more we think about an attack, the more tense the mind becomes.

If karate-do is "moving Zen," and Zen is the breaking of attachments to all things including thinking when we should be feeling intuitively, then karate-do consists of moving freely through intuition, with a clear mind unattached to fear, tension, or anxiety.

Zen and Buddhism call this clear, intuitive state of mind *satori*, or enlightenment. *Satori* may be achieved in many ways—through meditation, devotion to arts such as tea ceremony (*chanoyu*), flower arranging (*ikebana*), paper folding (*origami*), and so on. But in karate we call enlightenment "perfect timing," because it gives us a distinct advantage over enlightenment attained by other means: it gives us the ability, through strong techniques, to take advantage of our perceptions by counter-attacking when necessary. While Zen monks might be able to perceive attacks before they come, they might be powerless to do anything other than escape. While escape is always the preferred method of self-defense, it is not always possible. And karate techniques are for that once- or never-in-a-lifetime when no escape is possible.

It is for that one attack from which there is no escape that we train with utter commitment and perform techniques with totality—100 percent effort of body and mind.

A term frequently used in advanced karate classes is *hara*, and it may be translated literally, as "center" or "belly." Move from *hara*," we frequently hear. Or, "You have lost your *hara*! Concentrate! Find your spirit!" While *hara* does mean center, it does not necessarily mean "center of the physical body," and herein lies some confusion.

The physical center of the body is the *tanden* or *seika tanden*, an area surrounding the body's center of gravity and ideally located on an imaginary line between the navel and the tailbone. When instructors admonish students to tuck in the buttocks and abdomen, they are trying to make the student realize that the position of the center of gravity determines the body's balance. It should go without saying that poor balance always results in poor technique. Also important is the use of the large muscles of the hips and *tanden* for torque in developing linear and angular momentum. All body movements begin in the *tanden* because therein lie many of the largest, and potentially most powerful, muscles of the body.

Hara, on the other hand, implies "center of the being," or "center of the mind," or "central essence of feeling." *Hara* is that discrete force composed of *ki* (life force or vital energy), which makes our eyes show anger or joy or pity or grief. It is that unique property of mind that projects perception or confusion through the eyes. While the *tanden* is a specific part of the body, the *hara* should not be thought of in the same manner. While technically the *hara* is seated in the belly, it should be thought of as "feeling," full of energy, at once inside and outside the body. For example, if we are offended or angry and want to project that feeling to someone else, we can do so without verbalizing how we feel. Our attitude and demeanor make our feelings known. Without self-control, we do not keep strong emotions to ourselves, "bottled up" inside. When our feeling is projected to other people, it is no longer just inside us; it has spread to the outside, also. And this phenomenon is not limited to negative feelings; it also is manifested in love, joy, energy, and so on. When we project our feelings to others, it is because the particular feeling is consuming the major part of our thoughts at that moment.

By centering our feelings in the *hara*, through training and self-discipline, we are able to control our feelings and emotions and show them only when we want to. Even more than self-control, awareness of *hara* requires great concentration. If we can learn to concentrate fully on one thing and maintain that concentration under stress (attack), we will naturally develop great self-control.

Literally, *hara* refers to the stomach and abdomen and the processes associated with them. In Zen, the *hara* has two distinct points of reference for both physical and metaphysical functions. One is the solar plexus, and one is the *tanden*. Physically, the solar plexus is a nerve center that controls the processes of digestion, absorption, and elimination; the *tanden* is the ideal center of gravity.

From a metaphysical viewpoint, the bottom of the *hara* (the *tanden*) is the point at which the mind, body, and vital energy (*ki*) achieve equilibrium. When the mind and body are centered in the *tanden*, they radiate energy outward, in unison, like the spokes of a wheel or the petals of a lotus.

By centering the mind and body in the *tanden*, we can overcome nervousness (hunched shoulders, stiff neck, aimless thoughts), and achieve deep relaxation. The more relaxed we are, the broader and more open will be our scope of vision, awareness, and imagination.

In karate, we strive for the clear, intuitive state of mind in which the body moves freely. We use the *hara* to center our entire being—physically, mentally, and emotionally. And from the *hara* we extend our feeling out to include ourselves, our opponent, and the environment.

After years of training, we find that karate is a circle. What we strived for in the beginning (defense against surprise attacks) we return to after achieving physical mastery, and the cycle repeats.

The cyclical nature of martial art training is called *shu-ha-ri*. *Shu* (obedience) means learning from tradition; *ha* (divergence) means breaking the bonds of tradition; and *ri* (transcendence) means going beyond tradition to find something new.

> "After years of training, we find that karate is a circle."

While most of us remain in the *shu* stage for a lifetime, a few go on to complete mastery of physical technique, break away and try their own ideas, and ultimately transcend into the realm of a completely new technique or art. This is what Gichin Funakoshi did when he formalized karate and changed the *kata* to meet the needs of the Japanese. But Funakoshi found, as other have and will, that what lies beyond *ri* is *shu*: the original challenge of how to make a stronger stance, a stronger punch, a better person.

Thus, the final answer to "What is karate?" lies not in the shiny new black belt of the *shodan* (first degree black belt), but in the worn and tattered black belt of the master—the belt that is gradually returning to white, fulfilling the circle.

Zen and Bushido: The Great Empty Circle

The word, Zen, is a transliteration of the Chinese *chan-na*, which means "meditation." The concept of Zen was brought to

China from India by Bodhidharma, the first Buddhist patriarch to China, in about 600 A.D. Its arrival in Japan dates to the end of the 12th century, which coincides with the emergence of the warrior class at the top of the Japanese feudal system.

Only in the West are "experts" so ready to delineate the intricacies of Zen and tell us what it is. Indeed, the best description of Zen lies in what it is not. Zen is not a doctrine, nor a metaphysical philosophy, nor a psychological system, nor a religion. In the purest sense of the words, it has no rules, no ideology, no beliefs, no icons, and no temples. Its masters are not bound by dogma, nor do they enter into monastic vows. If we believe them, we accept that Zen offers no salvation and no condemnation. Zen does not proclaim a reward or a savior. At the same time, it makes no effort to deny us those beliefs as we see fit.

What Zen purports is that a person's life is like a knotted rope, and that it is better to untie the knots one by one than to add more. The knots exist as illusions or appearances, and they obfuscate the original nature of the rope—straight and smooth. If Zen has an ultimate goal, it is to see the essence of reality, to enter the "Void." But the Void of Zen is the opposite of nothingness. It is at once full, complete, and empty, like a great empty circle.

The spirit of Zen defies logic, reason, and analysis. It is, above all, direct awareness of reality through direct action. Zen rejects intellectualizing in favor of a flashbulb awareness of truth.

The Zen influence on Japanese culture commenced at the same time as the rise of the warrior class, and at first glance it seems paradoxical that Zen, the philosophy of passivity, should be adopted by the fearsome samurai and their descendants. But the Zen philosophy has two very appealing aspects for the serious fighter: (1) It calls for direct action without thought and without looking back; (2) It proposes that the enlightened person is utterly indifferent to life and death. It was, therefore, natural for the samurai to pursue Zen.

By the beginning of the 17th century, this pursuit led to a code of honor combining elements of Zen, Buddhism, Shinto, and Confucianism. That code has come to be known as *bushido*, "the way of the warrior."

Bushido developed out of the very old Japanese tradition of *giri*, which means "duty" or "personal honor." As a feudal society, Japan was imbued with the idea that each class of society had a different *giri*, and the higher the class, the more rigid the *giri*. Since the samurai were at the top of the social structure, it was natural that their *giri* be the most demanding. And since the samurai were warriors, it was also natural that their code be concerned with matters of life and death.

> "Bushido *developed out of the very old Japanese tradition of* giri, *which means* "duty" *or* "personal honor."

Since a fighter obviously will be better without a fear of death, the code of *bushido* developed with contempt of death as its central theme. For the samurai this was beneficial both in battle and in his social position. It made him the unchallenged guardian of the dignity of his class. That dignity consisted of loyalty, bravery, justice, integrity, benevolence, and self-sacrifice. All of this he sought to maintain through direct action in a state of *mushin* ("no mind"). That is, what is done is done according to the code of honor, but without consciously thinking about it.

This state of mind is symbolized by the two statues who guard the gates of many Japanese temples. One is Fudo, "The Immovable," and the other is Kwannon, "The God of 1,000 Arms." Symbolically, Fudo represents the fierce spirit of man, immovably rooted to the earth—fierce and unshakable.

Kwannon, on the other hand, is the God with 1,000 arms—each working in coordination with the others—capable of performing all of the necessary tasks.

Fudo alone would not be a sufficient guard because he is so strongly rooted and fierce that he would turn everyone away. Kwannon alone would be so involved with his many activities that he would be apt to indiscriminately admit too many.

Together, Fudo and Kwannon represent the enlightened person—the person firmly rooted in their code of honor and being, but able to unflinchingly perform their everyday tasks and duties with perfect coordination and without thought or worry.

The ultimate aim of true *budo* is for the body to perform its tasks without being distracted by thoughts in the mind, and for the mind to hold fast to its foundations, regardless of what events surround or permeate the body.

Thus, we may stand in even greater awe of the great karate masters who seem to retain and even increase their skills, in spite of advancing age and reduced training time. Their technical skill has become such an integral part of their being that it is completely divorced from any conscious efforts: Karate-do has become the person, and the person has become karate-do.

Karate-do and Personality

It is correct to assume that if one spends a great deal of time at an activity designed to improve character, one will experience changes in personality. Gichin Funakoshi's most famous quote is, "The ultimate aim of karate-do lies not in victory or defeat, but in the perfection of the character of its participants." This, along with the principles of the dojo (to seek perfection of character; to be sincere and honest; to show strong spirit in all undertakings; to practice courtesy; to control bad temper), has come to be universally recognized as the essence of karate philosophy.

But knowing just the essence of a thing does not imply total understanding. Indeed, in this case, like so many others, "a little knowledge can be a dangerous thing." It is especially important for instructors to delve more deeply into the meaning of character development as defined by *budo* philosophy, so they may better guide their students. All people attaining the black belt ranking should also study the subject more carefully to better understand and assimilate the psychological changes they undergo at advanced levels.

Very little has been written in English on the subject of karate's influence on individual personality. This is due in part to the newness of the art in the Western world, and in part to the inability of some Asian masters to relate the depths of karate-do to Westerners in an acceptable fashion. While we are able to grasp the essence of *budo* through training, the Japanese have no similar facility for grasping the essence of Western culture and thought without mastering the nuances of the language.

The culture from which *budo* arose was and is largely contemplative, while Western culture is largely utilitarian. It is not necessary to understand every detail or comprehend every fine nuance to benefit from Zen or *budo*. Clearly, it is far more difficult and exasperating for the contemplative person to absorb and assimilate the utilitarian minutiae, analyses, and configurations of the West. Again, Occidentals tend to want all the details so they can subjugate nature; their Eastern counterparts tend to want to glide smoothly along with the flow of nature, irrespective of details. We are trapped, therefore, in the middle of a natural conflict between the thinking of the East and the thinking of the West. And whether or not the Japanese masters are willing to acknowledge the problem, they are trapped in the same space.

We undoubtedly lose a great deal by not mastering the Japanese language; but we all lose far more by the Japanese not mastering English. The attitudes and beliefs of any society or culture are deeply buried in the society's language.

Nevertheless, we can learn a great deal by studying the Japanese writings of the masters and applying their thoughts to our daily training. The meditations of two past masters speak most clearly to us on the subject of karate and personality: the works of Jigoro Kano (1860–1938), the founder of judo, and Miyamoto Musashi (1584–1645), the "Sword Saint" of Japan. These two are selected because their writings speak most clearly to both the layman and the adept, and because each placed great emphasis on the ability of people to benefit from the philosophy of *budo* in general.

Kano, the great judo master, left us many volumes of writings. But in his last years, he distilled his thought on the value of *budo* into three basic precepts that have been handed down from generation to generation by his followers. They are:

1. *Jiko no kansei*—"To strive for perfection of character"
2. *Jita kyoe*—"Mutual welfare and benefit"
3. *Seiryoku zenryo*—"Maximum efficiency with minimum effort"

For Kano, *budo* was the basis of everything, but he recognized that each individual, even a great technical master, must consciously seek to make *budo* work for them, or they would gain nothing but physical strength.

The foundation of Kano's philosophy was that strength in one area, such as becoming a karate champion, gives confidence and leads to success in other areas, but only if we consciously seek success in those areas. If we do not consciously seek to apply the principles of karate-do to our daily lives, we will not change at all. Foolish braggarts who attain the rank of black belt are still, first and foremost, foolish braggarts, unless they consciously seek to improve their character and personality through their training.

Of course, one who stays with karate training over a period of years will develop courage, self-control, discipline, and awareness. But these are traits that may or may not accurately reflect the core personality of the individual.

The core personality is the abundance or lack of not just the traits mentioned above, but also health, intelligence, judgment, and moral rectitude. Kano's maxim of *jiko no kansei*—to strive for perfection of character—meant to strive in every area of life as if you were in the *dojo*. If something seems beyond your intelligence, approach it as you would a *kata* that you don't understand: break it down into pieces and methodically go over each piece again and again, until you master it completely. Seek guidance and help as necessary, but don't give up.

When you face a problem requiring good judgment, approach it as you would an opponent who is about to strike. Try to catch the "feel" of the situation with your intuition, and then follow through boldly. Poor judgment is usually the result of thinking too much about consequences. When we dwell on the possible consequences, we are dwelling on matters beyond our experience. And we know that what is beyond our experience we tend to fear and avoid. The *budo* way, on the other hand, is to make the best possible decision now and complete the action without further thought. This comes from our training: thinking about the consequences of the opponent's attack or our response always results in defeat. For the samurai, it resulted in death.

> "When you face a problem requiring good judgment, approach it as you would an opponent who is about to strike."

Budo uniquely speaks to the matter of moral rectitude without moralizing. The precepts of discipline, courtesy, humility, respect, and justice all relate to basic human morality without setting doctrinal rules that would cause damnation if broken. The keynote of morality in karate is justice. Gichin Funakoshi taught that the manifestation of a person's level of development in karate is seen in their commitment to justice. Similarly, in the writings of Miyamoto Musashi, justice and injustice are considered to be part of the natural rhythm and timing of things. The pure heart that seeks to do the right thing in each situation is the heart of the true master.

The morality of *budo* lies in the prevention of conflicts—all conflicts between human beings and conflicts within human beings. *Budo* literature is full of the concept that one whose heart and intentions are impure is defeated before beginning, but that one who is fully committed to justice will as readily go forward against 10,000 enemies as one if the cause is true. This thinking is supported by the fundamental Zen attitude toward death. The true karate master will act without hesitation for the cause of justice, without regard to the possibility of death.

> "The pure heart that seeks to do the right thing in each situation is the heart of the true master."

The second principle, *jita kyoe*, or "mutual welfare and benefit," speaks to the matter of compassion. This principle is not different from the Christian principle of treating others as you would like them to treat you. What is important to bear in mind is that compassion proceeds from a position of strength, and its virtue lies in the mutual welfare and benefit of those involved. Senior karate people (*sempai*) are expected to fight with compassion against their juniors (*kohai*). But this is more than just moving lightly; it is a matter of both people benefiting from the exchange. And how do the *sempai* benefit from such an exchange? They benefit from consciously recognizing that what they are doing reflects everyday life and from consciously studying the nature of compassion. By teaching, they also continuously re-learn the techniques.

Compassion always comes from a position of strength, but it is not true compassion if it is built on physical or material strength alone. The body weakens with age, and riches and positions may be lost. If people have not developed true compassion from a position of inner strength, they will receive no benefit when they need it the most.

When we are young and strong, compassion is an easy matter, but based on physical strength or position alone, it is not true compassion. In karate we must strive not to be haughty or condescending, but always to place ourselves in the position of student, knowing little and seeking a great deal. In this way, we can develop our personality traits on the foundation of inner strength and true character, regardless of our position or physical strength.

It is important and instructive to note that people who are truly strong and sincerely compassionate will be treated the same by people outside the *dojo*, who know nothing of their position in karate, as they will be by their *kohai* and peers.

Kano's third, and most often quoted, principle is *seiryoku zenryo*, "maximum efficiency with minimum effort." Anyone who has trained in karate for a year or two will instantly recognize the value of this principle in physical technique. In any physical activity, for that matter, it is best not to waste energy—to use only the energy and motion necessary to complete the task. In karate technique, the importance of relaxing and instantly summoning the energy and motion necessary to block and strike cannot be over-emphasized. Excess tension or thinking causes slow response and

results in inefficient techniques. This principle applies equally to daily life, where decisions must be made regularly. Indecision, worry, confusion, frustration, and guilt account for 90 percent of the energy and effort most people put into life decisions, but none of those factors will change the net result once the decision is made. We all experience these feelings to one degree or another, and how we respond to such stress strongly influences our personality. The philosophy of karate-do is that the energy and effort spent on these emotions usually is far more than the minimum required, and results are far less than maximally efficient. It is better, we believe, to acknowledge the negative emotions, but not to waste energy on them.

Using the best information at your command, make decisions boldly, with a clear, intuitive mind, and don't look back. If you later find, based on new information, that your decision should have been different, change the decision; but again, do it boldly.

This thinking is supported in whole by the long traditions of the martial arts: live fearlessly, live boldly, break attachments, die like the cherry blossom.

The second writer for consideration, Miyamoto Musashi, was Japan's most famous swordsman ever, and he is revered by the Japanese today as Kensei or "Sword Saint." Both the facts and legends of Musashi's life are well known to the Japanese people.

Musashi killed his first man in a duel at the age of 13 and was so invincible by the time he was 28 that he discarded his swords and defeated his enemies with *bokken* (wooden swords) or sometimes sticks. In at least one famous instance, he defeated a great master of the Shinto-ryu school of swordsmanship with a crude stick carved from the oar of a rowboat.

Unlike his contemporaries, Musashi lived through more than 60 duels and retired to die peacefully. In his later years, Musashi became Japan's premier swordsmith, sculptor, calligrapher, painter, metalworker, and woodworker. It was this amazing man who said that he came to understand the way of strategy at the age of 50 or so. He wrote, "Once you have attained the way of strategy, there will not be one thing that you cannot understand. You will see the way in everything." [1]

As perhaps the most famous man in Japan during his lifetime, Musashi consistently rejected riches and comforts. His humility was such that he spent the last two years of his life in a cave called "Reigendo." There he lived a life of quiet contemplation and wrote the *Go Rin No Sho*, the *Book of Five Rings*, finishing it just three days before his death.

We choose to study carefully the *Go Rin No Sho* because it is the master treatise of Japan's greatest warrior, the man around whom many of *budo's* legends and traditions revolve.

The *Go Rin* or five rings to which Musashi alludes are, according to Buddhist tradition, related to the five parts of the human body. Number one is the head, number two the left elbow, number three the right elbow, number four the left knee, and number five the right knee. These, in turn, corre-

---

1. Miyamoto Musashi, *A Book of Five Rings*, The Overlook Press, New York: 1974. (Translated by Victor Harris).

spond to the Buddhist *Go Dai*, the five elements of the cosmos: ground, water, fire, wind, and void. Accordingly, Musashi divides his text into five sections, each dealing with a separate cosmological element. He prefaces his entire work with three major precepts.

First, the essence of all *budo* is *kokoro*, which means "mind." Kokoro comprises the heart, soul, mind, and feeling (*ki*) of an individual and is reflected in the individual's manners and demeanor. Thus, when we say in karate, "*Mizu no kokoro*" (a mind like water), or "*Tsuki no kokoro*" (a mind like the moon), we mean that the whole essence of the mind, heart, soul, spirit, and feeling should be clear and reflective, like the surface of a pond, and see the whole environment like the moon, which shines down equally on everything before it.

The second great precept is that the strategy of *budo* must permeate our every action, both in the *dojo* and out, so that we may achieve *bunbu itchi*, "pen and sword in accord." That is, the firmness and steady spirit we gain in *budo* must be exhibited in everything else.

Musashi tells us that the way (*do*) is in all things, and we cannot attain the way if we remain ignorant. This further implies that there is no truth or understanding in the karateka who concentrates on physical technique only. The purpose of *budo* is to develop the whole person.

The third, and all-encompassing, point is the ultimate goal of "learning with no teacher." While we need a *sensei* to guide us, we must ultimately learn and understand by ourselves. No teacher can teach us how to feel, or how to have good judgment, or how to be moral, or how to be just. The teacher can only guide us and give us physical and mental exercises to help us find our true nature.

Zen philosophy says that we will find and recognize our true nature when we can see our "original face" (*honrai no memmoku*)—the face we had before we were born and even before our parents were born. This implies that the vital life force, *ki*, is pure energy, and can be neither created nor destroyed. It may change shape or form or receptacle, but it is always what it originally was—energy. To see their original face, people must look deeply inside themselves and backward beyond birth. In so doing, people find that they fit nicely with rest of the cosmos and that their emotions and desires are illusions ingrained in them since they were born.

"Original face" is sometimes called "original mind" (*honshin*), or "the true man" (*shinjin*), or "the mind of an infant" (*akago no kokoro*). By whatever name it is called, it implies an acute awakening of thinking (*kotsunen nenki*). It is a sudden realization of one's own identity, the realization of "one thought" (*ichinen*). It is as if another entity has come into being to direct one's actions, both in combat and in daily life.

This psychological phenomenon is known as "no-ego" (*muga*). It is at this point that the person and their technique become one; the person is karate, and karate is the person. There is no distinction between the two, and the "original mind" guides the actions, unencumbered by the body or mind.

Musashi says that when we can see everything in a broad scope and understand how everything relates to everything else, then and only then can we find the way. Later we will see that this includes studying small things and matters as if they were large, and large things and matters as if they were small, and from the juxtaposition of these opposites, come to know the truth.

It is interesting to note that while *budo* has employed this method of stimulating creativity and understanding for centuries, it is a concept not seriously considered by Western psychologists until the late 1970s. Since then, a growing body of scientists and doctors has been investigating the theory that it may just be this juxtaposition of opposites which, more than any other single factor, triggers creativity.

In the "Ground" book, Musashi talks of techniques and says that techniques are a "roadmap of the Way."[2] The key to this roadmap is timing. Timing is in everything, and there are different types of timing for different situations. Musashi says it is important to differentiate between active and passive timing (there is a time to move and a time to wait), fast timing for small things and slow timing for large things, distance and background timing (bring what you already know to the situation, and use your knowledge to perceive the right time to act), and off-speed timing (using timing the opponent does not expect).

We can easily accept that timing exists in all physical activities, but in *budo* we try to heighten our awareness and perception of timing and use it to our advantage not only in athletics, but in dancing, music, sex, and so on. The businessperson can use timing to influence gains and losses, and the employee can use timing to better manage workflow and responsibilities. Again, timing is in all things, whether we are aware of it or not. And this principle is not unique to Eastern thought, even though we are approaching it from the samurai point of view. The Judeo-Christian belief of "To everything there is a season" is in fact a very strong statement on timing.

---

2. Ibid.

While physical timing in karate may seem to be the most difficult to master, it is, if we follow Musashi's advice, the easiest. It is not sufficient to simply understand the timing of all things, but to control it. Musashi gives us nine broad principles and says that if we master these, "you will be able to defeat 10 men with your spirit." The principles are:

1. Do not think dishonestly.
2. The Way is in training.
3. Become acquainted with every art.
4. Know the way of all professions.
5. Distinguish between gain and loss in worldly matters.
6. Develop intuitive judgment and understanding for everything.
7. Perceive those things which cannot be seen.
8. Pay attention even to trifles.
9. Do nothing which is of no use.[3]

If these broad principles could be mastered, one could conceivably transcend all mortal problems and become superhuman. Of course, they cannot be fully mastered, but at the same time every person could begin to live by these principles and improve daily. The key to *budo* is the pursuit of these principles along with pursuit of excellence in technique.

The "Water" book speaks to the shaping of the spirit. Water is the symbolism because it always adopts the shape of its

---

3. Ibid.

receptacle and because it can flow at different speeds—sometimes as a trickle and sometimes as a tidal wave. Further, water is clear, which implies clarity of mind and spirit. In the matter of shaping the spirit, Musashi lists 12 major points:

1. Always maintain calm determination.
2. Meet each situation without tenseness, but not recklessly.
3. Keep your spirit settled and firm, but unbiased.
4. With the spirit calm, do not let the body relax.
5. With the body relaxed, do not let the spirit slacken.
6. Do not let your spirit be influenced by your body, and do not let your body be influenced by your spirit.
7. Do not lack spirit nor be over-spirited. Both are weak.
8. Do not let the enemy see your spirit.
9. If you are small in stature, know the spirit of a large opponent, and vice-versa; then do not be misled by the reactions of your body.
10. With an open and unconstricted spirit, look at things from a high point of view.
11. Cultivate your wisdom and spirit: learn public justice, distinguish between good and evil, study the ways of other arts one by one. When you cannot be deceived by men, you will have realized the wisdom of strategy.
12. Learn from battle to develop a steady spirit.[4]

Again, these are not principles that will be mastered tomorrow or next week or next month or next year. Perhaps we may never truly master them, but the point of *budo* is to try.

Also in the Water book, Musashi describes the methods of using stance, gaze, and arm position for cultivating the spirit. The point again is that the spirit is like water and adopts the

---

4. Ibid.

shape of its receptacle, the body. It is important to note that Musashi was describing sword fighting, but his principles of stance, gaze, and arm position are virtually identical to those taught in modern karate:

Principles of Correct Fighting Stance
1. Head erect
2. Forehead and bridge of nose unwrinkled.
3. Narrow eyes.
4. Slightly flared nostrils.
5. Hold the line of rear of neck straight. Instill vigor from the hairline down through the body.
6. Shoulders low.
7. Buttocks tucked in.
8. Strength in lower legs.
9. Brace the abdomen against your belt and do not bend at the hips.
10. Maintain combat stance in everyday living.

Principles of the Twofold Gaze
1. Gaze should be large and broad.
2. Perception is strong; sight is weak.
3. See distant things as if close, and close things as if distant.
4. Do not be distracted by insignificant movements.
5. See (perceive) to both sides without moving the eyeballs.

Principles of Position of the Arms
(The Five Attitudes)
1. Upper (*Jodan*)
2. Middle (*Chudan*)
3. Lower (*Gedan*)
4. Right Side (*Migi*)
5. Left Side (*Hidari*)

(Of these, the middle is the most preferred and effective.)

Musashi uses fire as the symbolism for actual fighting (*jissen*) because the spirit of actual combat must be fierce and burning. The underlying principle of actual combat, however, is to train day and night, under all conditions, ill or well, so that your spirit will remain the same, regardless of the surrounding conditions. In the Fire book, we read of the strategy of fighting (*sen, sen-no-sen, go-no-sen*) and how to use the *kiai* (a loud shout from the pit of the stomach) to get into the rhythm of the situation. But all of this amounts to nothing without a fierce, burning spirit.

The "Wind" book comprises practical advice about acquainting oneself with the techniques and training methods of other schools and styles. This study is not undertaken to learn how to defeat other martial artists, but rather to broaden one's scope and to find superior training methods.

Finally, the book of the "Void" is presented as having no beginning and no end. The Japanese character for the void is the same character used for the *kara* of karate and comes from the Zen principle of "rendering oneself empty." This means empty of illusions, false pride, false confidence, and intellectual commitments to psychological "systems" and "methods," all of which obfuscate the true nature of human beings. To live in the void is to live in tune with the laws of nature and to respond to any situation accordingly. To live in the void is to know intuitively the natural rhythm of the situation and to strike naturally.

The void is an expression of true karate: moving freely through intuition, with a clear mind unattached to fear, tension, or anxiety. We are born in the void, and we die in the void.

When we say that we practice our techniques until they become "second nature," we are also saying that we practice *budo* until we find our "true nature." When we can reach the intuitive state in which we learn our true nature (learning with no teacher), Musashi says, "Then you will come to think of things in a wide sense, and taking the Void as the Way, you will see the Way (*Do*) as Void (*Kara*)."[5]

> *"The void is an expression of true karate: moving freely through intuition, with a clear mind unattached to fear, tension, or anxiety."*

What we hope all of this will bring us to is a state called *myo* in Japanese. *Myo* is a creative and original force emanating from the unconscious, or from the "original mind." *Myo* is the state of the master who moves creatively and spontaneously from the unconscious, irrespective of technique or skill or universal concepts. It is the state of the spider spinning its web, the bee building its hive, the cool breeze blowing softly across the dew at dawn.

Myo is attained when the conscious mind delves deeply into the unconscious and perceives the void as all things and noth-

---

5. Ibid.

ing. In *myo*, the true nature of things is realized, and the lines between physical, psychological, and metaphysical are forever destroyed.

One of the most famous sayings in Japanese martial arts is, "*Myo wa kyo-jutsu no kan ni ari*," and it means, "The perfect, exquisite state (myo) lies between what is substantial and what is insubstantial."

> *"In* myo, *the true nature of things is realized."*

Such is the nature of *kara*; such is the nature of *do*.

Stress and Anxiety

It may be that stress and anxiety are the most deadly enemies of modern life. Before one can attain the deeper levels of karate-do, one must understand the nature of stress and anxiety and strive to calm the mind.

Just as strong emotions like joy and sorrow always manifest themselves in some part of our lives, anxiety also will manifest itself, in one form or another, in our bodies. Different people react differently to stress. Some develop ulcers, some skin problems, some heart trouble. The stress itself is the outer force that bears down on us and causes anxiety. Anxiety, in turn, plays a strong role in pain, allergies, obesity, heart disease,

learning disorders, speech disorders, sexual maladjustment, and mental illness.

Anxiety is a very unpleasant state of tension or uneasiness that arises from the mind's perception of stress as a danger to the body. When we fight against anxiety, we often over-react and cause both the body and mind to develop symptoms that indicate that a severe conflict is taking place. These symptoms often develop into neurotic and non-organic illnesses. This occurs because the body is well-equipped to respond to fear, fear being a reaction to a short-lived, external threat or danger. But the body is ill-equipped to maintain the fear response over an extended period of time.

Fear occurs in response to a specific stimulus, while anxiety is like a "drawn out" fear of something we cannot see or recognize or specifically define. When the brain perceives a threat, it "super-charges" the body's defense mechanisms and temporarily suspends a number of normal body functions. In fear, the heart beats faster, the blood pressure rises, and blood is redirected from the stomach and intestines to the heart. The spleen contracts and discharges its supply of red blood corpuscles to provide the increased oxygen necessary for the extra energy needed for fighting the danger. And the mind automatically decides to either escape from the danger or fight it. This is universally known as the "fight or flight" response.

In anxiety, these functions tend to occur on a more continuous basis, and the body inevitably suffers. Physical manifestations of anxiety frequently include extreme muscle tension, greatly increased energy expenditure, fatigue, fast pulse, high blood pressure, nausea, heartburn, aberrant digestion and elimination, and many others.

When we understand the potentially devastating effects of anxiety, we have no trouble deciding that anxiety is a feeling we do not want. Through the practice and study of karate-do, we can find release from anxiety and lead productive, vigorous lives, regardless of stress.

> *"Through the practice and study of karate-do, we can find release from anxiety."*

The basic karate method of achieving emotional strength and also overcoming anxiety involves strenuous training of the body and mind together.

Karate is, above all, a physical, dynamic, athletic endeavor. Only through hard training can the body and mind be brought into unison. All of the passive arts, such as yoga and meditation, have their benefits, but they are not enough to preserve our lives in time of danger. In karate, we can realize our own nature, clear our minds, and at the same time learn to protect our precious lives from destructive forces. It is not enough to

simply meditate on the nature of the universe and our surroundings; we must be concerned with the precious nature of our bodies and the life within them. Karate training can help in this respect. It may be difficult at first to correlate the ideas of gentleness, non-resistance, and courtesy with the medium of breaking bones, but that is where karate is, and it is where we must strive to be, also.

Even if we fully understand the nature of stress and anxiety, and even if we come to a piercing awareness of how to overcome them, we will not have gained much if we lose our lives to a mugger. No matter how much peace of mind we may gain through meditation or religious devotion, we will still have great problems when confronted with a violent attack. Direct attack is the most stressful situation possible for any person, and how we react at such times is a measure of our inner strength and our level of understanding.

What must be done is for the individual to face stress and anxiety in the controlled atmosphere of the dojo and learn first-hand what it is all about.

Karate is primarily a self-defense art, and as such, its method is to place practitioners in one stressful situation after another and teach them to cope. In the early days of karate development, the students were not students in the purest sense of the word. They were people whose lives were in danger and who were interested in preserving their lives and the lives of their families and friends. Each encounter was a life and death struggle. Punches and kicks were not practiced to win a tournament or to look pretty, but were practiced with the idea that not doing them correctly would result in losing one's life.

With this in mind, it is somewhat easier to understand why the old masters are still held in awe today. We sometimes think they were so proficient because they invented the movements. The truth is that if they were more proficient than we, it was because they were struggling for their lives.

In the *dojo* today, we do not think much about life and death when we train, and this is unfortunate. For it is in the life-death struggle that karate has its roots. The training must therefore be strict, disciplined, and at times severe.

Training in sparring and kata must be conducted with the utmost stress and commitment. Instructors must push their students physically to levels that the students think they cannot attain. In sparring, all attention must be directed to the life-death struggle, and the training must be deadly serious.

This is not to say that anyone should be hurt, but it is very important for advanced students to at least occasionally feel that their personal well-being is in danger, and that they can alleviate the danger by doing their techniques better, stronger, and more consistently. It is the job of instructors to instill in their students this feeling of seriousness.

> *"Attention must be directed to the life-death struggle, and the training must be deadly serious."*

Basically, the task is accomplished in the *dojo* by placing the students in a strenuous, stressful situation in which they place their trust in the instructor and seek to overcome the stress by trying harder. Basic sparring should not be done simply for the perfection of physical technique; rather, it should be done in such earnest and with such intensity that the students actually feel tense. When the correct block and counter-attack is performed in basic sparring, the students should feel a great relief and a sense of accomplishment.

The more advanced the students become, the more often they should be pushed by the instructor toward their physical limits. For the students who persevere, the limits will constantly expand. They will find, in time, that what troubled and exhausted them six months earlier is no longer a problem. They must be forced to feel danger and exhaustion, but they must not be allowed to become discouraged. Thus, each class should end on a positive note. If the students have been pushed very hard, they should be allowed to finish the class with something positive.

This fundamental karate training method is analogous to Aristotelian tragedy: the student must experience fear and anxiety, be allowed to overcome it in a controlled environment, and experience the feeling of relief that leads to confidence and emotional strength.

In this regard, it is the task of instructors to push their students hard. Instructors must show compassion but must realize that their main task is the development of strength and confidence in the students. Anything less than rigorous training cheats the students and gives them a false sense of confidence, which may put them in danger later. Sincere students must trust their instructor and realize that the instructor is severe not out of hatefulness, but out of respect for the nature of life and the desire for the student to learn how to protect it.

Samurai Strategy

Over the years, one question about self-defense has been asked perhaps more than any other: "Sensei, what should I do if I get in my car, and someone hiding in the back seat grabs me by the throat or puts a gun to my head?" The correct answer has always been the same: "If a mugger is lurking the back seat, don't get in the car."

This is not a facetious answer. The plain fact is that there is little or nothing anyone can do when caught in a certain situation. In the case of the attack above, there are certain techniques that could be executed against the attacker, but their success would require a high degree of awareness of lapses in the attacker's attention. A person who has such awareness would surely be aware of the danger before entering the car.

People who master karate-do will be able to defend themselves in any situation, but not on the basis of physical ability only. The most important aspect of self-defense is for students to understand their position at all times and become aware enough of themselves and their surroundings to be safe. Avoidance is always the best method of self-defense, but to avoid danger, one must be aware that the danger exists.

It is foolish to think that merely by training the body, one may be safe in any situation. Even the most skilled athletes cannot escape from a surprise attack if they are not aware of the attack until it hits. Once hit, the body may be too injured to respond. Therefore, the essence of karate self-defense is awareness of the attack before it occurs.

To more clearly understand this subject, one should consider types of attacks in two categories—surprise attack and contemplated attack. Contemplated attack is an attack that the defender perceives in advance, has time to think about, and responds to from a strong defensive position. The techniques and training of a first degree black belt are more than adequate to meet the challenge of almost any contemplated attack.

Surprise attack encompasses all types of attacks that are initiated before the defender is aware of them. Again, the skills of a first degree black belt are generally adequate to defend against many surprise attacks. The black belt usually will be able to nullify at least part of the force of an unarmed or armed attack due to superior reflexes, timing, and coordination. But these physical responses have their limits, and the parameters of those limits shrink with age. The goal to strive for is to relegate all potential attacks to the level of contemplated attacks. The method for doing this is the *do* of karate-do.

First, we must train the body to make it strong; then we must train the mind. Awareness is not a quantitative "thing" that can be learned; it is a state of mind that must be realized. The ultimate goal is to maintain a feeling of concentration in the *tanden* 24 hours a day. Using the *tanden* as a focal point, we may then proceed to develop awareness of the environment.

> *"Awareness is not a quantitative "thing" that can be learned; it is a state of mind that must be realized."*

Using the example of the mugger lurking in the back seat of a car, consider the value of training your mind to focus on the *tanden* every time you approach a car door. This is relatively easy to master. Simply take a few moments to place the image of the car in your mind. Visualize yourself walking toward the car, lowering your breathing to the *tanden*, and looking in the back seat. Visualize the back seat empty, and see yourself get in, calm and secure. Visualize an attacker in the back seat, and see yourself walking away calmly to call the police or seek shelter. It is not difficult. Then, when you actually walk to your car, do the same thing. You will find a keen sense of calmness and a general feeling of well-being. By concentrating on your breathing, you will feel no fear.

The aware mind is not paranoid. Paranoia is laden with fear, while the aware mind is devoid of fear. The simple exercise of looking in the back seat every time you enter a car will develop strength rather than fear.

Remember that we are not afraid that someone might be in the car; we are afraid that someone might attack us if we get in and that we would be helpless. Therefore, we can overcome that fear completely by not getting in.

Martial artists often refer to this kind of thinking as "samurai strategy." The samurai warriors placed the highest priority on one's position in any situation and the strategic use of that position for self-defense. In the case of the car, we should think of our actions in terms of "position." Being outside the car when we perceive the danger is the best possible position to be in: we can run and avoid the confrontation altogether. Being inside the car when the danger is perceived is a very bad position. If you get in the car and then realize that you forgot to check the back seat, turn around immediately and look. That would put you in a better position for defense than if you were driving when you perceived the danger. This kind of thinking is essential in the development of awareness for self-defense.

To take another example, assume that you have just entered a room full of people, most of whom you do not know. This could be a PTA meeting, a cocktail party, or even a theater. Someone you know calls out to you from the other side of the room and beckons you to come over. You simply walk through the crowd to your friend. Such a reaction is very bad because you are throwing away an opportunity to train your mind and heighten your awareness. Instead of mindlessly walking through the crowd, pause for a few seconds when you enter the room, and exercise your mind with samurai strategy. Drop your breathing to your *tanden* and first observe the approximate number of people in the room. Second, see where the exits are, and look at the windows to see if they could be used as exits. Third, observe whether people are in small groups or scattered. Fourth, consider the atmosphere: is it tense or jovial? What you are doing is determining your position in terms of self-defense. Samurai strategy is a diverting and pleasant game that helps develop a sense of well-being and increases your powers of observation.

If there is a large group of people between you and your friend, perhaps the best strategy would be to walk around the group rather than through it. Perhaps a small group is arguing and another is joking. It would be better to walk through a happy group, even if you have to walk farther. Perhaps no one calls to you. In this case, it might be better to take a position as close as possible to an exit. But be aware of what is outside the exit: an attack could come from that direction, also.

If you sit down, think about the chair in terms of self-defense. Is it a stuffed chair in which you would sink down and be unable to rise from quickly? Does it have arms that could restrict your movements? If it has arms the same height as the table it is next to, don't pull it up to the table and box yourself in. Will the legs of the chair slide on the floor, or will they stick? Is it possible to sit with your back to the wall? If you sit on a sofa, it is better to sit on the end so that you may not be attacked from both sides at once.

Consider the manner in which you sit. If you bend far over and grasp the chair with both hands to pull it to you, you are vulnerable to attack. Bent over, looking down with both hands behind you is a poor position for self-defense. Sit down straight, and maintain feeling in the *tanden*. Learn to sit and rise from center (*hara*).

Again, bear in mind that samurai strategy is a game, but it is a game that will become part of you and protect you from danger. As you exercise the strategy, forget about fear. Fear has no part in it. You are training your mind to be aware; you are not worrying about being attacked.

> "Samurai strategy is a game, but it is a game that will protect you from danger."

In its broadest manifestations, self-defense is not limited to personal defense against an assailant. In a larger sense, it is defense of the human organism against all threats. In this sense, self-defense includes the act of looking both ways before crossing the street. Through experience and training, we learn to be aware of the danger of crossing a street without looking. In a similar fashion, one does not slice a tomato by holding it with one hand and raising the other hand high over the head to quickly slash downward with a sharp knife. It is not that the tomato would not be cut; it is that we know better than to perform such a careless and dangerous act.

Practicing samurai strategy is merely a method for teaching us to be careful and prudent at all times.

It is most important that while playing the strategy game, you let no one know that you are doing it. It must be natural and private, so that it can become a part of you as you actually are, without pretense or affectation.

The goals of this exercise are similar to the goals of training a blind person. Blind people seem to hear better than the rest of us, but in fact they are simply more aware of sounds. Their perception of sound is heightened because they must rely on it more than sighted people for vital information about their surroundings.

> "Samurai strategy is a method of heightening all perceptions, and making the person less vulnerable to attack."

Samurai strategy is a method of heightening all perceptions, and making the person less vulnerable to attack.

The more you exercise your mind in this direction, the less chance you will have of falling victim to surprise attack.

The Karate Experience: A Way of Life

The singular distinction of a pure martial like karate-do is that its mastery bears direct applications to day-to-day living, personality, psychological stability, and survival. We know that the connection between training in the *dojo* and conducting the business of day-to-day life can be very strong, but it is important that we do not separate our karate training from our daily lives. If lines are drawn between karate-do and the business of everyday living, both disciplines suffer. Delimitation is alien to the spirit of Zen and karate-do, and if we believe in the spirit of *budo*, we also believe in the universality of all things in the cosmos. It should be noted, though, that it absolutely is not necessary for students of karate to practice Zen in a formal manner. What is important is to realize that karate-do, in its modern manifestation, arose from a culture strongly influenced

by Zen Buddhism and Shinto, and there is no question that those influences have helped to shape the thinking of the great karate masters who have developed and transmitted the art to others. Therefore, it is instructive to consider the great precepts of Zen in relation to karate-do and to scrutinize the possible impact of these precepts on our daily lives.

In Zen, we are encouraged to break our psychological attachments to "things" and especially to thinking and theorizing. In karate this is manifested in the strong emphasis placed on allowing the body to move freely through intuition. Thinking takes time, and time creates *suki* (opening). A pause in kata appears as a jerky, unnatural movement. In sparring it appears as instant defeat. In everyday living, too much thinking about the potential consequences of a decision results in frustration and anxiety. Facing a difficult life decision should be viewed in the same light as facing a skilled opponent: let your mind mirror your opponent (problem), and strike forcefully from *hara* the instant you sense the opening.

Zen also concerns itself with the nature of death, and tells us to understand death and then put it aside. In karate we perceive death as the fear to go forward, and we strive rigorously to prevent that fear from interfering with total commitment in technique. Once we perceive death and pain as natural eventualities, we can throw them out of our conscious being and perform our techniques boldly. When we have no thought for our own lives, we can become truly selfless in our relations with others. If we think about others, and not our own reward or penalty, we will act quickly, without hesitation or question.

Zen teaches us to let our minds move freely. In karate, this is encouraged by being open-minded to our *sensei*, our seniors, our peers, and our juniors. Students of karate must not become self-satisfied or rest on the laurels of their achievements. They must always try new techniques and seek new ideas and training methods. In the *dojo* and out, we can be efficient only if we relax and proceed from *hara*. Since a closed mind is a stiff mind, and a stiff mind cannot reside in a relaxed body, only those with open minds can completely relax.

By breaking our attachments to illusions through Zen, we eliminate doubt and suspicion. This is basic to the idea of *budo*, which means "to stop conflict." In the *dojo*, the elimination of doubt and suspicion is supported by the demand for complete trust and faith in the wisdom and experience of the *sensei*. When we are suspicious of the motives or intentions of friends or business acquaintances, it is frequently because we have not eliminated the conflicts in our own thinking. By trusting our partners in sparring, we learn that self-respect is the foundation of respect for others.

> *"By trusting our partners in sparring, we learn that self-respect is the foundation of respect for others."*

The calm mind strived for in Zen is developed in karate training by learning to withhold one's inner feelings from the opponent. The stable emotions gained in sparring and self-defense can serve the student well in any stressful situation. Through training we can learn how to center our emotions to overcome anxiety. When we can overcome anxiety associated with direct attack, we will find day-to-day stresses to be far less problematic.

As Zen teaches us to rely on our intuition, karate teaches us to concentrate on "feeling" rather than thinking. We are taught to develop our personal style from basic ideas and to understand the cyclical nature

of the universe (*shu-ha-ri*). By carrying this concept into our daily lives, we will be less perplexed by changes in our bodies and lifestyles and environments.

The master of karate-do tends to view happenings in a broader scope and perceives relationships between seemingly

disparate events. This reduces the natural, psychological resistance to change, and enables one to be more satisfied with the course and direction of one's life.

The practice of Zen results in increased sensitivity to the ebb and flow of the cosmos. Through sparring and self-defense, one develops great sensitivity to the feelings and intentions of the opponent; through *kata*, one develops sensitivity to one's own body and to the environment. Karate students also become more sensitive to the ebb and flow of *ki*, both in themselves and in others. Heightened sensitivity to how others feel is very beneficial in the development of any personal relationship. Further, in sparring we give and receive with complete sincerity, and following the same rule in daily life results in greatly increased understanding of how others feel when they are giving and receiving.

One of the greatest contributions of Zen to karate-do is the concept that what we see on the outside is a reflection of what is inside us. That is, fear of an opponent, for example, does not lie in the opponent, but only inside the one who is afraid. Thus, if we gain control over ourselves, we will gain

> "Fear of an opponent does not lie in the opponent, but inside the one who is afraid."

control over the opponent. In this regard we may say that actions are the mirror of the mind. What a person does reveals more about that person than what they say.

At the same time, the mind is the mirror of actions. That is, those who are truly modest and sincere in their minds will act modest and sincere in their daily lives. Those who feel inferior will work the hardest to impress others.

From these basic connections, we can begin to live by the precepts of our art, both in and out of the *dojo*.

The fundamental precept of character change and development is the same in any area of endeavor—karate-do, Alcoholics Anonymous, psychotherapy, religion, and so on—is that the individual must want to grow and change. No amount of discipline or work or counseling will help anyone unless they want it to help.

As Jigoro Kano pointed out, the martial arts will improve people only if they consciously seek to carry over the positive aspects of their training into their daily lives.

In karate-do, as in everything else, we must accept and remember that the rewards we reap from it are directly proportional to the effort we put into it. If we expect and seek improvement, we will obtain it; if we expect failure, we will fail before we even begin.

The Positive Lifestyle

Of all the "isms" conceived in the 20th century, none has had a more deeply felt and far-ranging impact on men and women than "assertivism." That we have felt compelled to coin this word to explain our past failures points irrevocably to our continuing failure to move out of our emotional defensiveness. If we accept the premise of psychologists who espouse assertiveness as the ultimate cure for everything from cancer to psoriasis, then we must also accept that the majority of us are a dopey, dithering, ignorant lot who would not recognize common sense if we died of it. From Freud to Fromm and from Esalen to EST, we are bombarded with propaganda that says, in effect, "You have a problem. You can solve it by getting to know yourself better. Come to us, and we will teach you how." What this really is saying to us is that we, alone as individuals, are not

capable of recognizing our own problems, much less solving them without a doctor or therapist or guru.

While it is true that people often need outside help, it is the premise of karate-do, as set forth here, that almost anyone (barring psychosis) is more than adequately equipped to recognize their own strengths and liabilities, and to be as happy and emotionally stable as they choose to be. All one needs is the desire to move forward with an open and receptive mind.

The *do* of karate-do nourishes the idea that it is better to be positive than negative. This message of karate-do as a way of life has had a limited impact in the West because of one great failing: karate-do was introduced by the Japanese as a macho activity, limited in scope to those men who must be tough, ultra-masculine, and brave. Perhaps this approach could work in the West if karate required a handgun in application. But since the techniques require a lifetime of hard work, karate-do has been relegated to the realm of the exotic, the eccentric, and the eclectic. Indeed, the admixture of karate and native American commercialism has often crossed the threshold of the bizarre. Impressed as we are by it, how many of us would actually want to appear half-naked on national television and have a watermelon sliced on our stomach by an Asian in carnival attire? That is not karate-do; it is not even karate-jutsu. Considering that a watermelon will split by itself when cut to a depth of three inches or so, it is not even a good show. Irrespective of the ludicrous theatrics, such demonstrations foster the impression that people who seriously study karate-do are all like the person holding the watermelon or the one holding the sword.

Since this crude commercialism shows no signs of abating, it is unlikely that in the near future karate will be taken seriously as an art with a high point of view by the public at large. Nevertheless, it is incumbent on Westerners who have some sense of the truth to spread that truth as far and wide as possible. When the old masters passed along their art to others, they did not do it for reasons of commercialism or profit. Virtually none of them was ever paid for teaching. Rather, they taught their art as an artist teaches a protégé. The art is passed on because it is a valuable and beneficial thing for people to have. Modern society, of course, operates on money. But far more important than making money and supporting a fancy *dojo* is the importance of living the spirit of karate-do on a daily basis. If the art will help people to live more peaceably, to gain good health, and to think more clearly, its propagation will be justified. If, on the other hand, it becomes purely a sport or a sideshow and contributes to frustrated masculinity and femininity, it should die, and probably will.

> *"The art is passed on because it is a valuable and beneficial thing for people to have."*

Idealism aside, the art of karate-do bears very important benefits for modern society.

First, it teaches us to distinguish between assertiveness and aggressiveness. Assertiveness is a matter of moving out of emotional defensiveness and expressing oneself in a clear, positive fashion, both in words and actions. Aggressiveness is over-compensation for insecurity, and it manifests itself in people who force their ideas and actions on another in a rude and obnoxious manner. Distinguishing between aggressiveness and assertiveness in someone is simple: if we don't like someone's attitude, they are aggressive.

On a larger scale, the development of a positive or negative personality is precipitated by how much of our attention we award to various kinds of behavior. In the *dojo*, for example, we learn to be aware of even the smallest movements of our opponent. But we learn to distinguish between movements that are designed to distract us and movements that are designed to destroy us. To do this effectively, we must become aware of the intention of the other party. If we once respond to a feint or an extraneous movement of an opponent during sparring, we forever will be controlled by that opponent; they will repeat that movement as often as we foolishly respond to it.

As art mirrors life, we learn from our training that people act toward us in a certain fashion because of the way we respond to their actions. When a husband shouts at his wife and aggressively dominates her, he does so because her response encourages him to do it. Perhaps he knows that his hatefulness is painful to her and that she cries privately in remorse. Her awarding of so much attention—so much crying and depression—to his foul manner is precisely the reason he continues his aggressiveness. Her response fulfills his basic human desire to be in control. A person who feels out of control of their own emotions can often derive great satisfaction from being in control of someone else's emotions. While we cannot hope to change the overall attitude of such a person, we certainly can let them know by our assertive response that we will not be controlled or intimidated.

Just as we do not award our attention to superfluous movements of the opponent in sparring, we can alter a domineering person's attitude toward us by asserting that we do not attach enough significance to their particular actions to be bothered by them. In so doing, we also are removing the essential element of any conflict—the opposition. If there is no opponent, there is no conflict.

From karate-do we learn to be direct without being caustic, as in sparring forcefully, but with control. We learn to be aware of the feelings and intentions of other people, and to determine whether they are angry, confused, or simply as direct as we are. We learn that fear of an opponent is just like emotional

> *"From karate-do we learn to be direct without being caustic."*

defensiveness, and we work hard to overcome it. When we coach others, we learn to express our ideas clearly, directly, and without digression or repetition.

Perhaps the greatest service paid to people who diligently pursue their art from a high point of view is the ability to focus on the other person. This implies a great deal. It implies that in this fast-paced, highly opinionated society, the sincere karateka can calmly and sincerely listen to what the other person is saying. By daily relating to all kinds of people in the *dojo* as peers, we can actually learn to acknowledge the value of another person's thoughts and ideas. Regardless of the type of individual we encounter in the *dojo*, we learn to form a bridge from our own thoughts to the thoughts of the other person. We find that, regardless of background or attitude or race or personality, everyone in the *dojo* is striving toward the same goals. If we

work very hard at it, we can perceive the essence of all conflicts between people as a matter of inflexible pride and aggressive ego. We learn that people can exist peaceably together without agreeing on every detail. As we move deeper into our art and start teaching others, we learn to be assertive in a positive fashion, without be aggressive or domineering.

When we can put aside our own thoughts and emotions and ego and pride, we can actively listen to what the other person is saying. The result of focusing on the other person is called self-confidence. If we are confident of our own ability to think and to reason and to act when necessary, we will be able to relate to other people without fear of rejection, without frustration, and without feelings of inferiority.

The entire process of character change and development in karate-do rests entirely on the desire of the individual to recognize and use it. In the *dojo* there is no psychologist, no therapist, and no guru. A good *sensei* is the embodiment of the literal translation of the title: "One who has gone before." Sincere teachers will push their students to their limits and beyond. The *sensei* must point the way to the correct path without interfering with the students' rights to be what they choose to be. Sincere students will follow the *sensei* and consciously seek to find the truth.

This is the path of enlightenment; this is the path of karate-do.

SWORD

Meeting Myself

Among karate people, there exists an unwritten code that dictates that we swap stories of seemingly inhuman feats performed by our instructors. Not only are these stories interesting, but they also bestow on the storyteller a sense of self-importance, as if by telling the story one obtains some of the skill of the masters. I have been as faithful to this code as anyone, and I certainly have witnessed feats that stir the imagination.

I have faced the great masters in free sparring: Hirokazu Kanazawa, Keinosuke Enoeda, Taiji Kase, Takayuki Mikami. I tell grand tales of Kanazawa standing 15 feet away and punching me before I could raise my arm to block; of Enoeda sweeping both my legs from beneath me, from behind (I never saw him move); of Mikami flinging me about the dojo like a yo-yo; and of Kase literally running over me as if I did not exist. My favorite, perhaps, is the tale of Hidetaka Nishiyama, the great JKA master, beckoning me to demonstrate sparring with him in front of the local television cameras. My whole life flashed before me as he executed a blindingly fast front thrust kick to my chin, stopping me in mid-charge. He held his foot there just long enough for my mind to register the impression of his toes against my lower lip. It was at that instant I decided that, given a choice, I would much rather be shot with a .38 pistol than hit by Nishiyama Sensei's foot or hand. Bullets, after all, leave the victim some chance of survival.

As exciting as my tales of wonder are, they really are pointless. I know they are pointless because some of my students now tell semi-fantastic tales about my exploits, and I have never done anything fantastic. I am still a beginner.

I would enjoy writing down all my fantastic tales for posterity, but that would deprive me of regaling my peers and embellishing the tales as necessary. What I will record here are stories of fact without embellishment. They flow through my subconscious like wind through a bamboo grove. They taught me then, and they re-teach me every time they appear.

Entering the Way

All 200 eyes in the room were focused on the slight man wearing the white uniform and black belt. The room became still as he bowed and slowly raised his arms in a wide arc, crossing them in front of his chest and extending them outward to the sides of his body. The stillness was shattered by the heavy thump of his arms suddenly moving in and out, destroying imaginary opponents. The snap, snap, snap held us breathless, spellbound, as the young man moved quickly through a different time continuum—punching, kicking, slashing—returning to us with a fierce shout that vibrated the air even after his body had returned to its original, quiet position. For several seconds, we forgot to applaud, forgot to breathe. Then we came down, clapping, stamping, whistling, and shouting. "What's his name?" someone yelled in my ear. "That," someone else shouted back, "is the great Kanazawa!"

I was stunned. Although I could not analyze it or explain it or describe it, I felt that something very important had just happened. I didn't know what it was, but whatever it was, it had jerked me away, for an instant, from my youthful righteousness and the street trauma of the hectic 1960s. Without reason or analysis, I wanted more. I wanted more of what I had seen, and I wanted to be what I had seen.

Hirokazu Kanazawa, then fifth degree black belt, was an All Japan Karate Champion who was making a world tour with his coach, Taiji Kase, and two other All Japan Champions, Keinosuke Enoeda and Hiroshi Shirai. They had come to the Midwest to show Americans what true karate was, and show us they did: Enoeda in self-defense against Shirai, the room quivering from the thunder of his powerful punches; Shirai driving Kanazawa backwards 30 feet with a furious flurry of kicks and punches, only to have Kanazawa leap high over the head of his opponent, kicking him in the back of the neck on the way down.

The barrel-chested Kase watched all of it impassively until it was his turn; then he flattened all three of the champions as they attacked him simultaneously.

I had been studying various styles of karate since 1960, and was proud to wear my purple belt, symbol of the intermediate rankings below black belt. But on that day, my mountain of pride was reduced to dust. We would all have a chance to train under these Japanese masters, and while we were eager, we were also plainly scared. But rather than beat us up, what they taught us over the next three days was what the "basics" of karate were. We learned about stability and the value of the long, low front stance. We learned to grip the wooden floor with our toes and to snap our hips forcefully with each movement. Again and again, endlessly it seemed, we would punch and kick, kick and punch. Snap and tense, snap and tense. When we reached that infinitesimal instant when the mind numbed and the body could no longer move, Kase's guttural scream would magically reach up to us from the earth and move our bodies against our wills. "*Hai*! Speed up!" Punch and kick, snap and tense, faster and faster we moved our limbs, our sweat-soaked uniforms crackling the air like static electricity. At the count of 10, we all screamed from our stomachs, "*Ei*!" or "*Osu*!" Then silence, and awareness only of the sweat pouring off our faces and wetting the floor.

I had tried other styles of karate: the high, light movements of Shorin-ryu, the cat-like movements of Goju-ryu, and the acrobatic spins and jumps of Korean Tae Kwon Do. Seeing the strength and beauty of this Shotokan style, I could not understand why everyone did not take it up. One of the masters explained, "The goal of martial art is perfection of human character, and many paths lead to the same goal. Because we have found the path that suits us does not mean that other paths are wrong."

Starting Over

I knew it was going to be a bad day as soon as I bowed. "No! Start over!" my teacher barked. I thought, Start over? All I did was bow!

The situation took place years ago, and my teacher, a great master, had traveled several thousand miles to see my students for the first time since I had opened my own *dojo*. I was surprised that, in front of my students, he treated me with great deference, as if I were a peer. For the first two days, he buttressed my confidence, talked intimately with me, and stroked my ego. By the second day of his visit, my ego was riding high on a wave of thick pride.

On the third and final day of his visit, he announced that we would each perform our favorite *kata* under his attentive and critical eye.

"You first," he said, pointing at me. "Everyone warm up."

Since I badly lacked regular instruction, I was ecstatic over the prospect of having my teacher give me a private lesson.

Standing on the floor in front of him, with all my students' eyes trained on me, I was ready to give them a show—to show them the excellence of my techniques. They would see why I had risen to a position of such high esteem in the eyes of the great master.

"Start over!" he growled. "You have no *zanshin*! Where is your spirit?"

My thought was one of embarrassment. Oh, well. My students probably wouldn't even remember such a minor error. But after bowing for the fifth time, I forgot about my students. I even forgot about the whir of the movie camera recording the fiasco. All I could hear was my instructor's harsh scolding. He and I were the only two people in existence, and my only desire was to perform the first movement of the *kata*.

"*Hai*! First movement! One!" he shouted.

Grateful for my release from torture, I performed that movement as it had never been performed before—smooth, graceful, flowing, strong, full of feeling and intensity. I could see an opponent in my mind's eye, and I could see him withering under the onslaught of my excellent technique.

"Oh, oh, oh," my teacher said, shaking his head sadly. "No," he said, adjusting my head. "No," he said, adjusting my arms. "No, no, no." He continued with my shoulders, my back, my legs, my knees, my feet, and my toes. Finally, he kicked my rump and whacked my belly—hard.

"Start over!"

And so it went, over and over, again and again, through each movement of the *kata*: me performing the movement endlessly, and my instructor whacking, smacking, thumping, and scolding. I must have completed each movement of that *kata* at least 10 or 15 times. As soon as I was able to perform it with some semblance of correctness, he would whack me and thump me again, shouting in my ear, "Start over!" And back to the beginning of the *kata* I would go.

For 45 minutes, we continued. No rest.

I'm going to pass out, I thought.

"Start over!"

I can't breathe!

"Start over!"

I can't see him! Where did he go?

"Start over!"

Suddenly I knew it. I knew it as well as I knew my own name: If he said "start over" just one more time, I would expire. I was going to die, and I didn't care. Anything would be better than this.

"*Hai*! Finished! Bow!" His voice came as gentle rain on a parched desert. It was over.

As I staggered toward the side of the floor, I saw the awed faces of my students staring at me, mouths agape. They were staring at the redness in my face, and they seemed perplexed by my ragged gasps for air.

They will probably all quit, I thought, now that they have seen how lousy I really am.

Then my teacher walked over to me, turning his back to the other students so they could not see his face. He patted me on the back, smiled, and very quietly, so no one else could hear, said, "Very good *kata*. I'm proud of you."

Returning his face to its steely scowl, he turned toward my students and shouted, "Next!"

Don't Run

When I was a brown belt, I started visiting a *dojo* where free sparring was practiced in every class. One of the brown belts in that *dojo* (I'll call him Clark) was particularly difficult to work with because no matter what anybody did, he would just run over them—literally run over them.

Facing him was like facing a bulldozer. There was nothing extraordinary about his technique, but if I shifted to the side, he would charge. If I shifted back, he would charge. If I stood still, he would charge. He even charged when I charged. It was very frustrating and resulted in many jammed fingers, jammed toes, and bruises from the clashes.

After being bashed by this guy one day, I approached one of the seniors in the *dojo* and asked, "What's the deal with this guy? He never backs up."

"Oh, he doesn't know how to back up," he replied seriously. "It's been erased from his memory."

He then told me that, until he reached the purple belt level, Clark had been the worst "runner" in the *dojo*. He had decent technique, but he

always ran like a rabbit when his opponent would charge at him.

One day the Japanese instructor despaired of telling him not to run and beckoned Clark to spar with him.

"Mr. Clark," he announced before starting, "do not run. You can do anything you want, but do not run."

When they started, the instructor stamped his foot, and Clark ran backwards. "Mr. Clark," the instructor said, "I told you not to run. Why you run?"

"I don't know, Sensei," Clark replied. "I'm really trying not to. Honest."

"Okay," replied the instructor, "I'll help you. From now on, if you run, I will hurt you. If you stand and fight, I won't hurt you, but if you run, I will hurt you. Do you understand?"

"*Osu!*" Clark replied, and they began again.

Of course it was only a few seconds before Clark was running backwards again, and the instructor motioned for him to return. They began again, and as Clark started to run backwards, the instructor followed him smoothly, grabbed the lapel of Clark's *gi*, and punched him squarely on the chin—a complete and perfect knockout.

As he gently lowered Clark's unconscious form to the floor, he beckoned to one of the seniors, and said, "Wake him up."

When Clark woke up and struggled to a sitting position, the instructor knelt down and spoke very quietly and evenly to him.

"Mr. Clark, I told you that if you ran, I would hurt you. You ran, and I hurt you. Now we are going to fight again, and if you move forward against me, I promise not to hurt you again. But if you run, I promise to hurt you more. Do you understand?"

"Yes, Sensei," Clark replied.

It is said that from the instant Clark stood up that day, he never ran from an opponent again.

A True Master

In the course of karate training, one has good days and bad days. At the beginning and intermediate levels, when students are still trying to impress their peers, it seems like one person's voice always rises above the din of the locker room after a training session. It is the voice of the lucky guy who had an exceptionally good day and was rewarded with the teacher's attention. His moment in the sun is always fleeting, and he generally takes advantage of it quickly and loudly. At least that's the way things worked in most of the *dojo* I trained in.

It is an exercise in pure egotism.

Such moments were rare for me, so I was doubly pleased when my chance came some time ago on one hot, July day. I was preparing to test for black belt, and my spirit was very high. Disregarding the humid, 104-degree Midwestern heat, the teacher pushed us hard for more than two hours.

The class began with hundreds of kicks and punches, followed by intense semi-free sparring with the emphasis on a new and difficult shifting maneuver. It seemed that everyone was struggling and stumbling—everyone but me. I was performing as if I had invented the maneuver. Even after spirit training—1,000 kicks with each leg, 100 sit-ups, 200 punches on the *makiwara*, 15 laps around the *dojo*—I felt fresh and energetic.

One of my seniors took notice of my energy, and he grabbed me by the arm immediately after class. "Let's spar for a while," he said.

Such an invitation by this particular senior was ordinarily not a coveted item. At six feet, three-and-one-half inches and 190 pounds, he was a giant in my eyes. My five-foot, six-inch, 130-pound frame was dwarfed by comparison. Not only that, but I was a brown belt, and he ranked in the second *dan*. We had a saying about him: "His arms are so long, I'll bet he can roll up his socks without bending over."

Nevertheless, on this particular day, I felt no fear, and it was a strange, new sensation for me.

We faced each other in the middle of the floor and bowed, and I immediately charged forward, propelled by a loud *kiai*, and punched him solidly in the chest. To my complete astonishment, he staggered backward and looked surprised. "Oh, boy," I thought. "That was the dumbest thing I've ever done. He'll kill me for sure now."

Again to my surprise, he didn't kill me at all. He charged toward me with one of his long legs lashing out in a front kick, but I magically shifted just to the side and punched him in the chest again. As he recovered, I drove my body forward, punching and kicking, and he actually retreated! "Incredible!" I thought. "Nobody has ever made him back up before!"

While this was flashing through my mind, our teacher suddenly yelled, "Stop!" Looking back at the incident now, I realize he probably stopped it before my senior became enraged and seriously injured me.

"Just like a tournament," our instructor said. "You two fight. I'll referee and call points."

We bowed again and circled each other cautiously. When I had faced my senior in the past, I had been filled with fear. But this time, it was as if there was a bright light illuminating his vital areas. All I could see was the "target" of his face, neck, and midsection.

He feinted with his front hand, and I drove in hard, slamming my fist into his belly and screaming a *kiai* from the bottom of my soul.

"*Waza-ri!*" the instructor shouted, indicating I had scored a half point. "*Tzukete hajime!*" he shouted. "Begin again!"

This time, my senior really charged fast and hard. As he did, I deftly shifted just out of his reach and, with my forward leg, snapped a roundhouse kick to his throat.

"Enough!" our teacher yelled. "Very good!"

We bowed, and my senior put his arm around me, squeezed my neck, and grinned. "You little son of a gun!" he said. "I didn't think you had it in you."

What a joy it was to strut into the locker room while all the other students dragged! My best friend, a student of equal rank, slumped on the bench in a sweating stupor while I bounced around the room, expounding, bragging, and explaining the details of techniques to all present, whether they wanted to hear it or not.

My friend slumped, expressionless, and said nothing.

For five or 10 minutes I continued. Still jabbering, I yanked off my belt and jacket, dropping my towel on the floor. As I stooped down to retrieve it, I cracked my forehead hard on a protruding clothes hook. Stunned, I bounced backward onto the bench a few feet from my friend. Seriously dazed, I sat motionless for several minutes. Gradually I became aware of blood trickling from my forehead and running down to my chin. Slowly, I turned toward my friend.

Still expressionless, he sighed, "Yeah, a true master."

Karate Ni Sente Nashi (There is No First Attack in Karate)

My senior (we'll call him Smith) was on his way home from the *dojo* one night when he was accosted by a youth wielding a billy club. Since Smith's car was in the shop at the time, he was forced to walk three miles to the school, which was in a very run-down part of town.

As he was walking, his would-be mugger stopped him, brandished a weapon, and demanded that Smith turn over his billfold. My senior politely but firmly declined to do so and stood ready to defend himself. As the youth swung his club in a roundhouse fashion, Smith blocked and counter-punched. The mugger dropped like a stone, but the force of Smith's block dislodged the weapon from the attacker's hand, and as luck would have it, the club flew hard against Smith's cheekbone. Nothing was broken, but his face was severely bruised, and for several weeks Smith had to answer the inevitable question, "Gee, what does the other guy look like?"

Some of us were discussing the incident in the *dojo* when our instructor walked by. Praising Smith's courage and ability, we applauded the fact that he was able to defend himself so well.

"You must be proud of him," one of my friends said to the teacher. "He controlled the situation very well."

"Stupid, stupid, stupid!" our instructor spat out in his broken English.

"But he defended himself well, didn't he?"

"No, no, no!" he raged. "This is a terrible example of self-defense. Smith-san not understand anything! He's just stupid! Let bad guy hit him like *makiwara* (punching board).

"Stupid, stupid, stupid," he muttered as he walked away.

None of us could figure it out. We just couldn't understand our teacher's attitude, so we decided to drop the subject of Smith's encounter.

About a year later, I was invited by another of my seniors (we'll call him Jones) to double date for a movie and dinner. After a pleasant meal, we were walking with our dates to a theater that was located on one of the busiest streets in the city. Suddenly, from out of the crowd there appeared a very big, very loud fellow who began shouting obscenities at my senior. The dispute, it seemed, was over the validity of Jones accompanying the young woman he was escorting that night. It turned out the loudmouth had been dating this woman for several years, but they had recently come to an unfriendly parting of the ways.

She was "his girl," the troublemaker was screaming, and he was calling into question the bloodline of Jones' entire family.

My senior quietly and patiently told the guy to calm down, that there was no point in making trouble, and that the woman had a right to date anybody she pleased. He then got close to the man and said very quietly, "Why don't you go down the street and bother somebody else?"

As the loudmouth continued to shout, Jones turned to me and my date and said, "Let's get out of here."

Since the loudmouth was pressing him very hard, I thought it odd that Jones turned his back on the guy to talk to us. Sure enough, just as my friend spoke to us, the troublemaker took a step toward him with his right hand raised. My impression was not that he was going to hit Jones. It seemed, rather, that he was going to grab him by the shoulder and spin him around.

But his intentions became irrelevant when, much to my surprise, Jones spun around with blinding speed, uttered a fierce *kiai*, and planted the hardest reverse punch imaginable in the loudmouth's face. The force of the blow snapped the man's head back and lifted him off the ground. He appeared literally to fly through the air, spinning as he flew, and landed face down on the concrete pavement with a sickening thud. He wasn't quite unconscious, because he rolled over on his back and groaned, clutching at his face, which was bleeding profusely.

"Now," Jones said quietly, again turning to us, "we can go to the movies." And he walked away, leaving the loudmouth rolling on the ground.

As this story got around the *dojo*, we all were certain that our instructor would be furious with Jones. He had a rule in his *dojo* that anyone caught fighting in anything less than an unavoidable self-defense situation would be expelled.

Inevitably, however, he caught a few of us discussing the incident, and we abruptly stopped talking when he approached.

"It's O. K.," he said. "I know all about it."

"Are you going to expel Jones-san?" some fool asked.

" Expel?" the teacher replied quizzically. "Why expel?"

"Uh, well, we just thought that the rule against fighting…"

"Rule say," he interjected, "anybody who fights when he can avoid, or anybody start fight, that person expelled. Jones-san O. K. He not start fight. He tried to avoid, had no choice. Must fight. Did good job."

" But," I asked, "Jones-san hit him first. What about *karate ni sente nashi*?"

"Ah, see," he replied, "you are stupid like Smith-san. Smith-san waited for guy to swing stick, and he get hit. First attack is not physical. First attack come when bad guy asked for wallet. Smith-san have bad strategy. He waited for guy's second attack. Jones-san, however, realize that first attack was when guy jumped out and started cussing. He tried to talk him out of it, but guy insisted on fighting. Jones-san just use good strategy: turn back and get bad guy off guard, then counter-attack. One punch, fight over. Question is not 'what is *karate ni sente nashi*?' Question is,'*what is first attack*?' Jones-san very smart. He understood."

If a Nail Sticks Up, Hammer it Down

For as long has I can remember, I have always loved to talk. According to my mother, I started talking at a very rapid rate when I was six months old, and my mouth has been active ever since. It is a pleasurable habit that has served me well in times of need, such as in school when I had not the faintest idea what the teacher was talking about. When called upon, I would scan the book in front of me, summon my best facial expressions, and pour out phrases laced with key words from the material at hand. That is what I was doing when my instructor caught me lecturing a new student in the locker room one day. He listened for a few minutes and then said, "Enough talk. Let's go."

Throughout the class that followed, I continued to talk to the beginner, correcting his stance, explaining the meaning of his training, and so on. Near the end of the hour, my instructor called me up to the front of the class and asked me in a loud voice, "Mr. Hassell, do you like girls?"

"Uh, well, yes, *Sensei*, I do."

"Do you have a girlfriend?"

"A girlfriend?" I asked, thoroughly bewildered.

"Yes, Mr. Hassell. I'm speaking English. A girlfriend."

This is a test, I thought. Speak crisply to the *sensei*. "Yes, *Sensei*, I have a girlfriend," I shouted.

"Do you ever arm wrestle with her?"

"Do I what?"

"Mr. Hassell!"

"No, *Sensei*! I never arm wrestle with my girlfriend!"

"Good!" he shouted." You are so weak, she would beat you! You are the most terriblest brown belt I ever see! All talk! No action!"

"Thank you, *Sensei*!" I replied crisply.

" You are welcome," he replied. "Get back in line."

To this day, I listen closely and speak very little when my seniors are present.

Haragei—Speaking from the Gut

Several years ago, one of my younger students accompanied me to a national conference of karate leaders. I told the student that paying close attention to the proceedings would help him understand the inner workings of a large karate organization as well as its Japanese and American leaders.

My student took my advice seriously and hung on every word in the day-long meeting.

Near the end of the meeting, a detailed discussion was held about a delicate public relations matter. My teacher, who was chairman of the meeting, spoke heatedly in Japanese with some of the other instructors, while the rest of us also offered our comments. Finally, someone proposed that the chairman be allowed to handle the difficult matter and that I draft a letter to the individuals involved. There were no objections to this proposal, but I noted my teacher was silent during the discussion and voting.

When the voting was over, I looked directly at my instructor and said, "Sensei, is this the way you want this matter handled?"

"Yes" he replied, looking directly into my eyes for several seconds. Once or twice, his eyes blinked rapidly.

"*Hai*!" I said, indicating that I understood.

When my student and I got back to my hotel room, we went over our notes from the meeting.

"When are you going to draft this letter and statement for Sensei? Do you want to do it now, or wait until we get back home?" my student asked.

"I'm not going to draft it at all," I replied. "Sensei said he doesn't want it done that way. I'll have to wait until I can talk to him alone to find out how he wants it done."

"But I distinctly heard him say yes when you asked him about it," the student protested.

'He said yes," I explained, "but he clearly meant no. I saw it in the way he blinked."

Reflecting on the incident, I'm sure my student thought I was crazy or had been to one too many meetings. But I was not confused. I was correct. When I talked to my teacher later, he explained the different approach he wanted to take on the matter.

What my teacher had said to me with his mouth was contradictory to what he said to me with his belly. The Japanese call this *haragei* (stomach art or belly talk). The Japanese people can say one thing but mean something entirely different. *Haragei* is the method of communicating by gut feeling, facial expression, length and timing of silence, and interpretation of seemingly meaningless sounds like "ah, ah, ah" and "eh-h-h-h...."

Haragei grew partly out of the well-known Japanese distrust of straightforward communication, and partly out of the racial, cultural, and social homogeneity of their society. After being raised with the same values for the past thousand years, they can be reasonably sure of their neighbor's reaction to any given situation.

By virtue of our great cultural diversity, Americans are taught to be specific. *Haragei* can be a source of great frustration to Americans dealing with Japanese karate instructors, but the problem is by no means limited to karate.

In his excellent book, *The Japanese Mind*, Robert Christopher tells the story of an American journalist who collided with *haragei* while interviewing an elder statesman of Japan's ruling Liberal Democratic Party. He asked the old man how many months it would be before the Prime Minister would be forced to resign. The statesman wanted the journalist to have the correct information, but he did not want to be quoted. So he turned to *haragei*.

Repeatedly muttering, *"Muzakashii ne,"* ("difficult question"), the statesman used his finger to trace the number seven on his desk top.

The American journalist, a long-time resident of Japan, got the message. But such has not always been the case for many American karate people who have met their Japanese counterparts in political settings. The communications gap has contributed greatly to a continuing rift between karate leaders from both countries.

The problem, however, could be alleviated if American karate leaders learn to look to their Japanese counterparts not just for the answer, but for the *haragei* behind the answer.

Discretion is the Better Part of Valor

In the 1960s, many karate people were arrogant when it came to comparing their style of karate to other styles. *"Dojo*

storming," a practice common in Japan before the 1960s, was carried over into many American *dojos*. What it consisted of was the members of one *dojo* showing up—sometimes announced in advance, sometimes not—at rival *dojos* and joining the class. The ostensible objective of this was to exchange training ideas. The real objective, of course, was to show the other guys how much tougher than them we were.

I remember one case in which the instructor at the *dojo* in which I was training set up an exchange training with a rival *dojo*, and we all ended up in a marathon physical fitness contest: They would lead in 100 squat-kicks; then we would lead in 100 push-ups; then they would lead in 100 sit-ups; then we would lead in 100 fingertip push-ups; and on and on.

Among all the ridiculous things I have done in my life, that kind of activity must rank in the top two.

Once, though, I remember it being fun.

In the mid-1960s, four of the premier All Japan Champions of the Japan Karate Association made a world tour and stopped off in the Midwest to give demonstrations and help us with our practice. A rival *dojo* at the time (a *dojo* for which we had no respect because they dressed in colored uniforms and engaged in what we believed were "weird" rituals) had stormed us a few weeks before the champions visited and had left us so sore and stiff that we were all a little reluctant to return the favor.

The instructor of our *dojo*, however, couldn't wait to pay them a visit, and he suggested to their instructor that we bring along the Japanese champions to make it more interesting.

When we arrived at the rival *dojo*, we all dressed out and milled around on the floor, flexing our muscles and stretching. As our rivals came out on the floor, we realized that we had not seen all of them before. There seemed to be a lot more of them, and they all seemed to be bigger than we had remembered—huge, in fact.

By the time we were ready to start, there were about 40 people on the floor—15 of us and 25 of them. We were on one side of the room, and they were on the other.

Just as our nerves were about as jangled as they could be, one of the Japanese champions noticed a leather, double-end striking ball, suspended from the ceiling and anchored to the floor, in one corner of the *dojo*. He approached it curiously, poked at it with his fingers, and bounced it lightly back and forth with his elbows. When he had everyone's attention, he suddenly, dropped into a long front stance, shouted a fierce *kiai*, and punched the ball hard.

Perhaps the ball was old, or perhaps the strings that kept the leather closed around the rubber bladder were not tight. I do not know. What I do know is that as the ball reached the limits of the rubber cords securing it, it loudly exploded, and the bladder flew out and bounced wildly across the length of the *dojo* floor. The champion, a sheepish look on his face, chased it down, picked it up, and handed it to one of the monsters on the other side of the dojo.

"Berry sorry," he said, as he bowed.

Five minutes later, 20 people lined up to take the class under the Japanese–15 of us and 5 of them.

We never did figure out where those other guys went.

If It's Non-Contact, How Do You Know It Will Work?

In the mid–1960s when karate was still a relatively new thing in America—a time when karate tournaments were largely a last-minute hodgepodge mixture of every Japanese and Okinawan style imaginable. When all these different styles got together, the leaders would sit down for a few minutes and agree in principle on the rules of the event. Detailed rules were left to the innovative discretion of the referee and judges during the contest.

I had fought in many tournaments as a white and green belt, but this tournament was something special. People were there from all over the Midwest, and some of the biggest names in early-60s karate were there to judge. A couple of them even entered the black belt sparring division.

The prospect of facing some of those big names, even though I was sure I would lose, excited my competitive brown belt soul. After much haggling and outright begging, I was allowed to compete in the black belt division. The tournament director seemed amused at the thought of a brown belt trying to compete against the black belts.

"Sure," he grinned. "Have at it."

The only rules that seemed etched in granite were no contact to the face, and no open-hand techniques to the face. A minor infraction of either of these rules would result in a warning, and two warnings would result in a foul and disqualification.

My first two matches went well, I thought, and I was surprised that I won them. My third opponent, however, was something else.

As I stepped into the ring, I found my five-foot, six-inch, 130-pound self facing a six-foot, three-inch, 180-pound ogre. He was an Okinawan stylist who apparently was more than a little miffed at the sight of this cocky little brown belt beating up on black belts. He glared and frowned at me, and to this day, I'm sure I heard him growl.

My teacher, it should be noted, had refused to participate in this tournament in any way. He didn't approve of "open" tournaments where the rules were not fixed beforehand. He had told me he did not want me to participate in this "circus," as he called it, but that if I insisted, he would go along to watch and take me to the hospital if necessary.

As I looked at the giant in front of me, I was pierced by cold fear. As I looked beyond him, I saw my teacher taking up a seat on the sidelines, folding his arms across his chest and staring at me with no expression at all. He knew what I did not know at the time: the referee of the match was my opponent's instructor, a man who also was not pleased that a brown belt was denigrating the black belt division.

As the match began, I dashed forward instantly and planted a reverse punch squarely in my opponent's chest. To my amazement, the referee said nothing. As the match continued, the big guy moved this way and that, punching and kicking almost continuously with his front leg. As he raised his leg for yet another kick, I shifted inside, grabbed his leg at the calf, and punched him solidly in the chest. The force of my blow, coupled with a heavy tug on his leg, sent him reeling backward onto the floor.

"Half-point!" said the referee disgustedly. Then he walked up to the face of my opponent and said something to him that was inaudible to anyone else.

"Continue!" he shouted.

Again, I dashed in with a punch to the chest, but no point followed. I punched once more, a little harder, but again the referee made no move to call a point. I looked at the referee, and he just glared at me with a smirk on his face. That smirk told me the whole story. There was no way I could win this match.

Angered by this blatant "fix," I charged my opponent with all my might. In a rage, I grabbed his uniform near his collarbone, and I punched him three or four times in rapid succession, very hard.

"Stop!" commanded the referee.

As I let go and dropped my hands, my opponent lashed out with an open-hand attack directly to my face. I think it was a palm heel, but I half turned and half ducked, and it caught me square on the side of the head, between my left ear and temple. As I spun around, he kicked out at me, landing a hard strike to the inside of my left thigh, narrowly missing my groin.

"Okay," the referee said.

I staggered back to my starting position and instantly became aware of three things: I could not hear out of my left ear, I could not see out of my left eye, and blood was gushing from my right nostril. The man had hit me so hard on the left side of the head that blood was coming out of the right side of my nose!

As the referee prepared to motion for us to continue, I held out my right hand, covered with blood, and looked at him incredulously.

"Oh," he said with nonchalance. "You want to quit?"

Stunned, I looked past him with my good eye and looked directly into the eyes of my teacher. With a sigh and a shrug of his shoulders, my teacher looked directly up at the ceiling, then back at me, and then at his hands, as if he were checking his manicure.

"No way!" I replied, wiping the blood on my *gi* jacket.

"One warning for showing disrespect to an official," the referee announced, pointing at me.

I bowed to him and faced the monster again. This time, as he moved forward, he did so with a very hard kick that caught me again high on the inside of the thigh. As he put his leg down, I grabbed his jacket and punched him hard in the face and harder in the body. As he reeled backward, I swept his feet from under him and hit him hard on the back of the head, bouncing his forehead against the wood floor of the gymnasium.

"Foul!" cried the referee, and it was over.

It took almost 30 minutes for my nosebleed to stop, and I couldn't hear out of my left ear for more than two hours. My eye turned very black and remained that way for almost two weeks.

My opponent, as it turned out, suffered a broken tooth and three broken ribs.

"And what do you feel now?" my teacher asked as I reached the sidelines.

"Ashamed," I replied, mopping blood and trying to feel if my left eye was indeed still there.

"And why did you not kill him?" he asked.

Shocked by his unusual question, I replied quickly, "Oh, I didn't want to kill him. I just wanted to get even. It wasn't fair."

"Hmm," said my teacher. "Maybe you are not so stupid anymore." And he walked away.

I realized that my opponent and I could just as easily have killed each other. As it was, we just made fools of ourselves. But when we hear the question now, "How do you know it will work?" we just smile and say nothing.

Use Your Brain
(When You Are Supposed To)

During a clinic, the instructor I was training with at the time asked one day, "Are there any questions?" Several hands went up along with mine, and he patiently answered all the questions except mine.

"You are too stupid to understand the answer," he said.

Later in the same month he asked me to attend a meeting of advanced students and instructors during which, after he outlined a complicated plan about an administrative matter, he again asked, "Are there any questions?" But I had learned my lesson well and silently stared at the table in front of me.

"Mr. Hassell," he said, "don't you have any questions?"

"No, Sensei," I replied, "none at all."

"You are stupid!" he shouted. "You are willing to just sit there like a lamb going to slaughter and let me lead you down the path! Use your brain for a change!"

Now I Know

In good karate *dojos* today, people do not get beat up or grossly humiliated, and they are never in fear of losing their lives. But among some of the Japanese instructors in the 1960s, the actions that today would result in lawsuits were then merely everyday training methods. Some of the Japanese instructors had not yet reconciled themselves to the fact that America is a land of team sports and that Americans, by and large, will not accept severe, individual torture, no matter how worthy the cause. Consequently, many talented people were driven away from karate.

Some of us, however, had begun training at a very early age, and we simply did not know that most people would not submit themselves to the kind of pressure we took for granted. And it was from that severe, individual pressure that we gained some of our deepest insights.

I clearly remember the instant I began to understand the essence of karate-do.

As was my custom, I had driven 250 miles to spend the weekend training with the only Japanese instructor for the JKA in the Midwest at that time. I was an 18-year-old brown belt at the time, and my ego was in full bloom.

We would arrive at the *dojo* around midnight each Friday, and would begin training at 10:00 a.m. Saturday. Saturday

training always continued until 4:00 or 5:00 in the afternoon, and we generally spent the evening visiting other *dojos*. One *dojo* regularly showed Japanese films until midnight on Saturday. When we watched these samurai movies, we would get inspired and go back to our *dojo* to practice. Since we had no money, the instructor would let us sleep in the *dojo* on the bare wood floor. Invariably, we were so exhausted by 2:00 or 3:00 a.m. that the hard floor was no inconvenience at all. And our youthful vigor made it easy for us to rise for five or six more hours of training on Sunday morning.

But on this particular Saturday night, the instructor walked into the *dojo* at 3:30 a.m. and loudly instructed us to get up and practice our *kata*.

Although thoroughly bewildered, we obediently got up, put on our trousers, and started practicing while the instructor beat the *makiwara* into oblivion. There were only two of us, and we kept giving each other questioning looks. What is this all about? we wondered.

After a half hour or so, the instructor told us to face each other for free sparring. We had been fighting lightly for a few minutes when he stopped us and said to me, "You don't know how to block. Anyone could punch you in the face. The only feeling you have for your face is fear."

He then had me stand in natural stance while my friend performed lunge punches toward my face. Again and again he punched, and each time I shifted and executed a rising block.

Basic sparring? I thought. This is silly. How can I show him my strength if he won't let me fight?

Gradually, my left arm became heavy. I was tired, and my forearm ached.

"No! Same arm!" the instructor barked, as I shifted to block with my other arm. "Now, harder! Faster! Stronger!" he yelled at my friend. Soon I was breathing very hard. Sweat blinded me, and the whole left side of my body felt as if it were being hit by a sledgehammer. Harder and harder my friend punched, until I was sure I was going to cry. Finally, I staggered backwards and literally begged, "*Sensei*, please tell me what I am doing wrong!"

Shaking his head in disgust, he turned to my friend. "This fella wears a brown belt and acts like a baby. Punch harder! If he doesn't block, hit him! Now!"

This time I moved fast, but my arm was just too tired, and I ducked, desperately trying to avoid the inevitable. **Bang**! I thought for an instant that someone had slammed a door. But then the pain exploded in my head, and I knew my left eye was black. It was tearing. In fact, both eyes were tearing. Against my will, I was crying.

"*Sensei*, what am I doing wrong?"

"Quiet! Hit him again!"

Bang! This time it was my upper lip. I was bleeding.

"*Sensei*...!"

"Again!"

Bang! My nose was bleeding.

I literally ran backwards, crying, "*Sensei,* please tell me what I'm doing wrong!" My whole body felt like it was on fire, and I was terrified. I really wanted to die.

With inhuman speed, the instructor charged up to me, his nose almost touching mine, and screamed, "If I tell you, you won't know!"

He stayed there for what seemed like hours, his glaring eyes burning into mine. It seemed like time stopped.

After several minutes, he turned and walked back to his original position. My tears were gone, and I felt no pain.

In complete silence, I walked back to my friend and bowed. He punched, and I blocked, perfectly. After several more minutes of silent observation, the instructor bowed and left the *dojo*.

Photographs

Japanese Temple, Kyoto, - 0, 3, 6, 15, 21, 23 - (Courtesy of Jose M. Fraguas)
Zen Garden, Japan, 5, 9, 11, 19, (Courtesy of Jose M. Fraguas)
Buda, Japan, 13 - (Courtesy of Jose M. Fraguas)
Suzuko Nakae, 16 - (Courtesy of Jose M. Fraguas)
Kanku Dai Kata, 22 - (Courtesy of Jose M. Fraguas)
Gichin Funakoshi, 26 - (Archives of Jose M. Fraguas)
Chokin Motobu, 29 - (Archives of Jose M. Fraguas)
Chojun Miyagi, 30 - (Archives of Jose M. Fraguas)
Chosin Chibana, 33 - (Archives of Jose M. Fraguas)
Gichin Funakoshi & Mel Bruno, 35 - (Archives of Jose M. Fraguas)
Nei Chu So, 37 - (Archives of Jose M. Fraguas)
Toshiaki Maeda, 39, 42 - (Courtesy of Jose M. Fraguas)
M. Gustavson & Steven Casper, 41, 89 - (Courtesy of Markus Boesch)
Y. Konishi, 46 - (Courtesy of Jose M. Fraguas)
Morio Higaonna, 49, 76 - (Courtesy of Jose M. Fraguas)
Meitoku Yagi, 50 - (Archives of Jose M. Fraguas)
Jose Egea, 53, 108 - (Courtesy of Jose M. Fraguas)
Kenwa Mabuni & Gichin Funakoshi, 55 - (Archives of Jose M. Fraguas)
Yashunari Ishimi & Tsuguo Sakumoto, 56 - (Courtesy of Jose M. Fraguas)
Les Safar, 59, 90 - (Courtesy of Jose M. Fraguas)
Randall Hassell, 60, 87, 95, 105, 121 - (Courtesy of Jose M. Fraguas)
Masahiro Okada, 62, 67, 113 - (Courtesy of Jose M. Fraguas)
M. Gustavson, 65 - (Courtesy of Markus Boesch)
Teruo Chinen, 68 - (Courtesy of Jose M. Fraguas)
Y. Konishi & Kenwa Mabuni, 71 - (Archives of Jose M. Fraguas)
Randall Hassell, 74, 125 - (Courtesy of the Author)
Y. Konishi, 78 - (Courtesy of Jose M. Fraguas)
Jorge Romero & Jose M. Fraguas, 81 - (Courtesy of Jose M. Fraguas)
James Yabe, 82, 84, 92, 124 - (Courtesy of Jose M. Fraguas)
Kenei Mabuni, 96 - (Courtesy of Jose M. Fraguas)
Kenji Sakuro, 98 - (Courtesy of Jose M. Fraguas)
Hirokazu Kanazawa, 101 - (Courtesy of Jose M. Fraguas)
Jorge Romero, 116 - (Courtesy of Jose M. Fraguas)

Notes